SCANNER

The Science of Hidden Language

Includes

Mind reading for business success

and Whistling giraffes.

CLIFF EDWARDS

Scanner - The Science of Hidden Language

Published in the United Kingdom by:

REAL Publishing
11 Mills Spur, Old Windsor
Berkshire, SL4 2ND, UK
www.realise.org

First printed September 2007

Layout & Design – Design Inc www.designinc.co.uk
Illustrator – Nicholas Biggs
Design Assistant – Chloe Jarrett

ISBN 978-0-9556010-0-2

It ain't what you don't know that
gets you into trouble.
It's what you know for sure that
just ain't so.

MARK TWAIN
(SAMUEL LANGHORNE CLEMENS)

Contents

Is communication more than data?

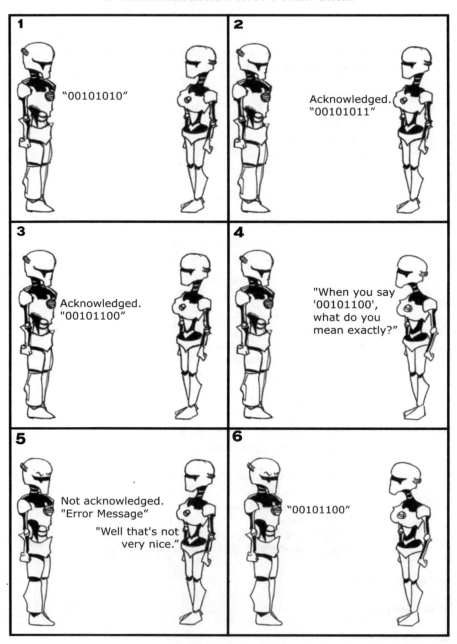

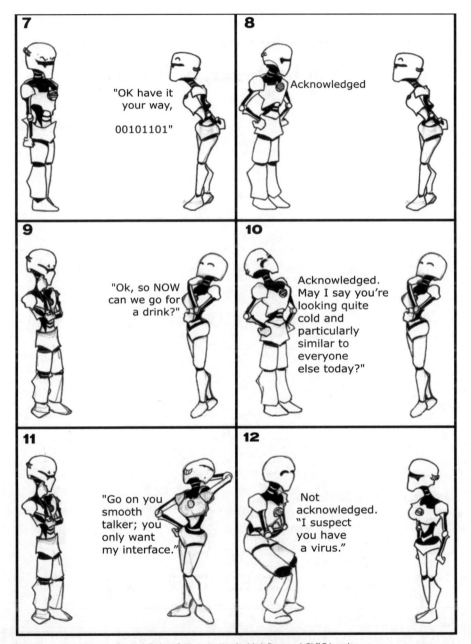

Figure 1, Robot Communication by Nick Biggs and Cliff Edwards

A man is but the product of his thoughts.
What he thinks, he becomes.

MOHANDAS GANDHI

SCANNER

THE SCIENCE OF HIDDEN LANGUAGE
(Reading People)

The tools and techniques of negotiators, interviewers and
managers that help them to understand others quickly and reliably.
It is also for anyone else who might enjoy added
insight into other people.

The unconscious of one human being
can react upon that of another without
passing through the conscious (of either).
S Freud

Figure 2 Contradiction

Introduction

Language, including body language, is symbolic; it represents a communication, as such it is often ambiguous.

The purpose of this book is to increase the reader's accuracy in predicting the motivation of individuals and groups and how they are likely to operate.

It will describe how much of human behaviour, thinking and reaction is structured.

It is designed for working professionals - managers, facilitators, interviewers and negotiators. It covers specific and practical models of personality and thinking in depth rather than a broad theoretical work covering the whole of personality and behaviour (That has not been successfully achieved since William James 'Principles of Psychology' in 1890.)

Scanner is able to access thinking because the meaning of our behaviour is intimately linked with the person's perception and memory. Although no one action can tell us what that action means about the inner workings of a person, by energetically observing, with an open mind, repeated behaviours in context we can begin to be confident that we are getting the hidden messages, even if the person doesn't know they are sending them.

It is my belief that amid an apparent chaos there is a universal **underlying** structure of MIND or, if you prefer, THINKING. Scanner is a set of tools and insights that help us to understand that structure and to improve how we deal with people.

People might seem complex; picking apart even one person to find out how they function seems like it might take a lifetime. However, we all already have exceptional brain structures designed to recognise and address social behaviour. These are capable of automatically noticing and classifying social issues in others and bringing them to our conscious attention. That process is vastly improved if we first study the structure of minds in the social context to back up the automatic systems we have.

This then enables our 'out of conscious' process to organise the observations better. As a result we begin to be open and to be aware of a deeper, more accurate, ability in recognising how behaviours are organised in others. We can begin to scan for differences and repetitions that have significance; hence the name Scanner.

> *Scanner is a set of practical tools and insight into people structures. Anyone involved in creating agreements with others will find those tools invaluable.*

Scanner is about people reading for the serious practitioner; it will not cover what it means when someone folds their arms, or scratches their nose as discrete acts. Scanner is about what works from real life experiences and sound research. It addresses the significant advances gained in people reading techniques, mainly developed over the last 20 years.

The reader will be offered insights into the way people display their true intent and needs. To become fluent you will need to reflect, checking the relevance for you and to integrate the tools into your existing methods.

A wealth of professionals have contributed: negotiators, recruiters, managers, psychologists, legal professionals and coaches. I believe these contributors will also benefit from the single structure provided by bringing it all together into a single causal process. Scanner makes our work more certain, fairer and removes much of the guesswork from people assessment.

This Scanner introduction lays the theoretical ground work and offers the means to practise the skills. Scanner can also give insights into group behaviour - 'Scanner the practitioner'.

Scanner is founded on many years working in organisations at all levels.

As trainers and psychologists, we found we needed to understand the structure of mind and how it affects behaviour in order to broker deals, reduce conflict, reconcile groups, effect social and organisational change and give career advice to individuals.

Many of our clients feel more in control, create better more lasting agreements with others and feel a lot less stress when they know how others are likely to react on the key issues that concern them.

We developed the science of scanning with help from our clients and colleagues in order to improve communication and so to give serious caring professionals an advantage in a world where the application of power is often with those who seek power for its own sake. It is clear that those with even a few of these skills are at an advantage. We believe that making these powerful skills available to everyone will help to level the balance of power.

Scanner helps to answer questions like, "Will they support my work? Agree with me? Like me? Understand? Who else will make a difference? Who might block progress?"

As we integrated Scanner into our work it seemed to be highly valued. The everyday feedback from our clients, that we were succeeding in forging effective and workable deals between parties and reducing unhelpful conflict, finally prompted us to write this book, a working manual for negotiators, interviewers, managers and business owners.

Research in cognitive, developmental and social research have produced significant insights over the last 20 years and we wanted to integrate these, where appropriate, into our work.

While conducting the research we looked for existing books that covered the interaction between mind, environment, personality, social context and behaviour. The relevant books, references and articles we found were: too detailed, inaccessible, trivial or so general that they gave no practical useful tools.

There were some useful Practitioner books the reader might like to reference: 'I Know What You Are Thinking' by a US Trial Lawyer Marc Mogil; 'How To Read And Use Body Language' by Jaskolka; 'Body Language' by Allan & Barbara Pease and 'Body Language At Work' by Clayton. However, they are mainly concerned with physical activities and are either culturally specific and/or open to interpretation. We knew we had to integrate body language, spoken language, causes of behaviour, social drivers, learned behaviour and a host of other issues to truly give the practitioner a science and certainty, reducing guesswork to a minimum.

Only by doing this could we hope to produce a real manual of hidden language. One book stood out from the rest; Julius Fast's 'Body Language': although primarily concerned with visible body language it could usefully be read as a precursor to this work. In addition, 'Man Watching' by Desmond Morris is very accessible and well researched.

Scanning is a multi-dimensional dynamic process; this book is a description, a translation of real world effects. As a cookbook cannot explain the taste of a cake adequately, to understand and use scanning, it has to be experienced and practised. Having a manual for a car or a musical instrument can only be really understood when one is in the car, Scanner comes to life when one is peacefully observing people and using the tools.

If you want to understand the nature and source of behaviour so that you can be better prepared for whatever negotiation arises, however unusual the clients are, this book has been designed for that need and I welcome your feedback on it.

editor@realise.org

GUARANTEES?

There are no absolute guarantees with people reading; everyone is unique and it is important to be clear about what Scanner can and can't offer. Body language and non-verbal language are, like all symbolic systems, even the spoken word, full of ambiguity. Scanner does not guarantee the evidence needed will be present. Scanner does show ways that can be used to elicit evidence if you are not seeing/hearing it. It offers certainty; **IF** we get the evidence and use it properly we are **confident** of our conclusions. We can become confident with practice, energy and skill.

WHAT'S NEXT?
Scanner Practitioner, the practice.

Scanner – an introduction to reading people. The follow up will be 'Scanner Practitioner', which will contain exercises to hone sensitivity, refine theories, models and processes to enable the better application of human modelling. In addition we are providing courses for Scanner Introduction and Scanner Practitioner and a web space to build a support resource,
www.realise.org/scanner

Courses

For information on Scanner courses, the experience and accelerated coaching see
www.realise.org

Email: admin@realise.org
Contact:Training Services. 44 (0)845 2255774

Other books:

Business Pragmatics – Get it done, in life and work
(People concepts for real people in business)

Planned

Rhetoric *– Verbal Manipulation.*
Dealing with put downs, shut outs and sarcasm.

Being *– Think Yourself into Being.*
Listening, thinking, problem solving - A route to understanding
(includes Eyes, Brick, Flower, Tree, Everything Squared, Nothing, Convergence).

Scanner Practitioner *– Applying Original Mind.*
(Exercises to increase scanning skills and capacities)

To Shep...

I dedicate this book to the person who has taught me most of the useful things I know about living in this social world, who has shown the most patience with my ignorance of the human condition and been the most challenging human being I ever met. My partner Sue Shephard. "Ditto".

I wish she could live forever and bring the joy, the nonsense and sense of silliness and fun she has brought me, to the rest of the world, especially to our beautiful children.

Acknowledgements

Thanks to:
Frank Farralley, Alan Schoonmaker, Tony Vinelott who demonstrate that you can genuinely respect people and still be tough.

Thanks to the staff at Starbucks Staines who laughed, provided coffee, and made me feel welcome, the names I know are: Ali, ZamZam, Bernie, Raj, Dina, Anthony, Eva and Emily.

Inspiration
Carl Rogers – "The Client Has Everything They Need", Carl Jung – Mental Life, Fritz Laing – Real People, Simons- Artificial Intelligence, Desmond Morris – People Watching, Eric Fromm - "The Art Of Being," John Norman- Introduction To Programming, Roger -Philosophy Of The Infinite, Banda Ji- "To Try And To Serve", Sue Knight- "It's true for you", Sister Elaine McKinnis – "Just Be" and "Mu", Rickman- Brilliant Pig Ignorance, Dr John- "Notice What You Notice", Aileen T – Gentle Strength and "What Are You Like?", Paul M - "You're Just Saying That Because It's True" and The African Lift, Peter S – Patience, Mum and Dad for the challenge.

So many people have helped to create the work, it would take a book to list them all; to you, thanks for making life fascinating. In addition I would like to thank those who consider themselves to be my enemy. I believe you helped me to learn and made me stronger, may you also experience the learning I had from you.

Common sense ain't common.

WILL ROGERS

WHAT IS SCANNER?

Chapter 1

WHAT IS SCANNER?

(Background)

PURPOSE

To give a context for Scanner and background to the psychological position, philosophy and a brief explanation.

OUTCOMES

On completion of this chapter the reader will be able to:

1 *Describe the assumptions on which Scanner is based*
2 *Explain the purpose of Scanner*
3 *Position Scanner compared to ordinary Body Language*

METHOD

A basic description of the background assumptions, models and theory of mind.

Warning!

There is a lot of theory at the front of this book, if you prefer, pick a chapter of which you like the look or sound and start there. Come back to the first chapter if you take an interest later.

THE HUMAN MACHINE

Our minds drive our actions and the mind seems to be constructed in the brain. The brain is a network of cells that act as complex (electric) switches. These cells can change the strength of their links to influence how charges move around the brain network, which in turn changes our thinking and behaviour. Our brains somehow store and update our models of the world including relationships from simple to complex. If we change the models we change how we perceive the world and how we act. Yet most of what we do is preprogrammed (Eagle & Pentland Structure in Routine).

For thousands of years great thinkers have wondered how this mechanism can produce an individual person; how the mind comes into being from a physical process. Some, e.g, behaviourists, might argue there is no mind, only a brain in action, and this is a continuing debate.

Because the mind is both **Associative in nature** and **Logical in structure**, many believe it is chaotic and those who prefer one way of thinking to another often find themselves at odds, even in heated rows, with those who are accustomed to thinking the other way. There almost seems to be a war between those who prefer simplicity, direct connections, thinking serially and those who think along many lines at once (network thinking), who more often understand the world through inference and social complexity. When differences are debated, seen as complementary rather than right or wrong, it produces deeper thought, not a decision or a hard truth, rather an intellectual tolerance of difference accepting possibility on all sides.

I will start from an assumption that when we meet someone we are communicating with a social individual in a social context, a pretty unique person with choice driven by beliefs, models, needs, understandings and social 'enculturation'.

For our purposes we will regard the **mind as an emergent property of the brain**. When the sea moves it creates waves, we all agree they are there and the power can be devastating. Yet there really is no such thing as a wave, it is a word for the way water can move; we call that an emergent property of water and energy working together. In the same way the brain functions and as a result produces perception, thought and action. Inexplicably our sense of self emerges from the working of the brain.

Because the brain is a network of connections it is less chaotic than it might first appear. Theoretically, if we could repeat the same experience exactly the same way twice, the brain would respond in the same way. However, we cannot freeze the state of a brain; it remembers and may respond differently to the same situation the second time. However, some discrete processes seem to act very similarly each time.

To establish what these are, I want to lay some foundations of the structure of thinking; that is, the brain in action.

Scanners are interested in what processes we can predict and are useful; what tends to work most; what processes can we observe and use to understand the needs of others.

Thinking in this brain is by association. As an area of brain is stimulated by a sound, image, feeling or thought, so too are areas that have, in the past, been stimulated at the same time. Areas of the brain become 'associated' with each other. A network of 'close by' ideas. You might think of it as electrical leakage. The power going along the main route, 'the route of least resistance', leaks along less well-associated byways to other groups of cells.

This is a possible explanation for an effect known as **'Signal Anxiety'**. The person becomes aware that they are feeling anxious during a conversation or event even though the conversation hasn't directly addressed anything fearful or the event is not yet dangerous. In the past they have come to associate an innocent event with something fearful. They 'expect' to feel dread. NLP techniques can reduce this 'inflammation' around an idea and so cause the client to become more comfortable with situations. See also "Spreading Activation" and "Parallel Activation" in Appendix 3.

For a Scanner these links become clear in prejudice, fear reactions. If our client reacts badly to a specific word we try to find a different way of saying the same thing. If they find noise distracting or a time of day difficult it may be physiological or a set of experiences. If every time you had an accident it was on a Wednesday, you might be fearful of leaving the house on Wednesdays, however irrational that might seem to others. We knew one client would never meet us at Runnymede in Surrey and we found another venue. He never said anything about the place, it just seemed he would avoid agreeing a date until it meant meeting elsewhere. After some time working with him, we found he had a (common) fear of the number 13 and Runnymede is at Junction 13 of the M25 motorway. It is not relevant that we accept a client's fear, however, if it prevents you working easily with the client, you need to be aware of it.

In addition to these developed differences we are constructed differently from conception. Research seems to suggest individuals operate their brain's switches (neurons) with different levels of background energy and this helps us to know how to present information; fast and with interesting asides to low energy brains and clear, structured without deviation to high energy brains. This has very little to do with intelligence in the normally accepted sense.

In many cases we can see that one person prefers to be quiet rather than be in noisy surroundings, while the other is happier in stimulating environments, with perhaps noise or energetic images.

Another preference of our brain that may be given at conception is the frequency at which our brain cells can fire. If they can replenish themselves quickly after they fire, so they are ready to fire again sooner; that person may have many more firing neurons. They are likely to have many associations being made as we talk with them; they may seem nervous. Alternatively, if their cells reset themselves slowly then the person may seem very stable, even slow or reluctant to evaluate all alternatives.

There are tools in the market like MBTI (Myers-Briggs Type Indicator) to help people to understand some of their preferences. Generally we are not able to ask people during negotiations to fill in a questionnaire, although that would be really helpful, so we have developed means to pick up on their preferences from observation.

When people with differently responding brain hardware meet, it can be stimulating or frustrating for them.

Although some of these preferences are given at conception the developing person adds coping mechanisms and hundreds of other preferences by experimenting with the world, even in the womb. By the time a child is five years old they have thousands of processes to help them to deal with their world.

Hans Eysenck describes trait development forming out of the meeting of the child's basic structure at conception and their reaction to the world in which it needs to thrive - Nature meets Nurture. The child arrives in both a physical and a social environment and it is usually well equipped to exploit it. So our task becomes slightly easier if we can differentiate between the person's given behaviour preferences and those they built up to cope.

Some people use relatively few models of the world to get by; others continually update their models. Noticing any extremes in this area can help us to work much more effectively with that client. The tools of Scanner include mechanisms to induct and test the patterns used by others so that we can work more effectively with them.

Scanning begins by listening with all senses, even using our own mind preferences, tools, models and states to 'notice what we notice'. To be an effective Scanner there are three main areas to study:

1 *Knowledge*
2 *Tools*
3 *Self state management*

This book will give the reader much of the knowledge, many of the tools and offer some exercises to get you started on state management. State management takes practice and we have utilised ideas from professional negotiators and interviewers, NLP and Zen to help us in that practice.

NLP – Neuro Linguistic Programming.
Created from their work with leaders in people development by John Grinder and Richard Bandler et al. It is the study of the structure of subjective experience, it contains methods for modelling, deriving the essence of other's behaviours and codifying those so that they can be used by others.

An experienced Scanner works with identity models, using metaphor because these tend to be the most effective. It is about accessing the person's drivers and needs that are beyond today's income or the next task.

For instance, many find they have climbed a 'ladder of success' only to find they put their ladder on **the wrong house**. It seems the choice was based on other people's beliefs and expectations – they are, as it were, nearing the top of someone else's house (parents, sibling pressure, spouse, managers). They sometimes feel empty, even wasted. At this point many embark on a process of self discovery.

Maslow (1908 - 1970 ref. 1998) called this rejection of unchallenged beliefs and the search for personal meaning **'self actualisation'**. People begin to ask:

> **"What do I need to fill me up?"**

Metaphorically their task becomes one of finding **a house to climb with deep purpose.**

The good news about this is that they may have some excellent ladder climbing skills, that they developed climbing the wrong house. Some realise it is the climbing they like, rather than the other assets of achievement. Are you more a journey person or more an arriving person?

Scanners can often become aware of the client's true purpose before the client is aware of it. This can help us to understand their conflict and to deal with their apparent contradictions.

A practical side effect of Scanning is that it enables us to profoundly accept the essential person without the need to measure their performance in any field. We are able to value them without their doing anything for us. The effect this can have on people is often invisible and empowering. It is as if someone has said to them, "OK, you are accepted unconditionally, so what are you going to do now, since you don't have to do anything to prove yourself any more?"

Although any conversation with almost any human being, if they are patient, can be valuable and healing, Scanner is not about counselling. Scanner is about gaining clarity. It has been used exclusively as a business tool. It may have many principles in accord with counselling – self reliance, the client has choice, some non intrusive questioning, these are an essential part of business transactions in general.

We invite you to read this book from a position of **"What can I use?"**, rather than "Is this true?". We built Scanner on what works and our tools have proven successful in the real world.

> *An important task for a Scanner, is to discover how a person organises their perceptions to deal with the world.*

The sources of motivation in people are varied: experiences, models, metaphors, beliefs, prejudices, organisation, expectations, contradictions, anxieties, strengths, weaknesses, desires, needs, hopes and dreams. A Scanner is trying to understand these drivers in others to better engage with them and to produce successful, lasting outcomes.

Man will do many things to get himself loved, he will do all things to get himself envied.

MARK TWAIN

BASIC SCANNER

Chapter 2

BASIC SCANNER

(FIRST TOOLS)

PURPOSE:
To introduce the reader to the observational processes of analysis,
understanding and persuasion of others.

OUTCOMES
On completion of this chapter the reader will be able to:
1   Give a description of Scanner
2   Give examples of channels of communication
3   Describe the process of observation
4   State the source of understanding in scanning
5   Describe the process of elicitation
6   State three sources of research that support Scanner

METHOD
A description of the formation of identity programmes
followed by observation.

**WHAT IS SCANNER? It is a process, a philosophy, a set of practical
tools and a profession.**

It contains: tools, processes, theory and theology (beliefs), ethics, practice, courses,
coaching. In learning and practising Scanner, the practitioner will inevitably come
to a point of understanding the structure of mind and personality. Therefore, in a
very profound sense, Scanner is also Self-Development and development of Self.

This book will focus on the practice of Scanner in the business context. We are planning books to explain the philosophy and ethics, which are not covered in this book: 'The theory and philosophy of Scanner' - Life please - hold the theory.'

Scanner is a series of tools and techniques that enable us to get quite detailed reliable information about someone else.

Scanning is a process involving detailed observation of behaviour in others using archetypes and interaction, leading to pragmatic descriptions of their behavioural preferences. This knowledge can then be used to understand their motivation and to help us to predict what they need and work with them more effectively.

2.1 Calibration (Triangulation)

For us to know the relevance of any behaviour we need to carefully observe the

Calibration – Everyone is different in a similar way

person in both an active and resting (quiescent) state. By 'resting state' I mean when they are not aware that they are being observed or not feeling or thinking anything extreme. We then need to notice deviations from that resting state; that is, which actions link with which states of mind. In this way we begin to calibrate the person. It is like setting zero on a temperature gauge. One way is to put the gauge in a place where we know the temperature is 0° and mark the gauge where the needle is pointing at that time with 0°, then put it in a place that we know is at 100° and mark where the needle is pointing now with 100°. If the needle moves consistently we can then mark all the other temperatures between 0° and 100° evenly.

We need to know the usual behaviour of a person, so that we can notice when that changes. We can then begin to collect evidence of what each change from a resting state means.

Everyone is very different, although there will be tendencies for people to act in certain ways in certain circumstances, we ought not to rely on these assumptions about universal behaviour. So noticing what is out of place is key to knowing the true state of the person being observed. If we are to notice what is out of place or unusual then the first step is to know what is usual for the person or group.

For 'quick and dirty' calibration or for large groups we use images of exemplars; see Chapter 6 Style, Typologies section iii Archetypes.

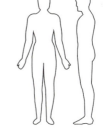

Imagine an archetypical standing person and keep that image in your mind. Now notice how your target person differs.

This helps to show up subtle differences like more pressure on one leg, various tilts which may illustrate intention, interest, alertness, back problems etc.

Figure 3 Body Outline

Figure 4 Mirrored Posture

Figure 5 Posture (Istockphoto Inc.)

Of themselves, they mean little, but if we notice a change at the same time that the focus of a conversation changes it helps us to build up a translation set between their inner thoughts and their behaviour. E.g, in the pictures above notice that the person on the left leans in on the forward step, while the other leans out. She is not intending to go forward yet, her weight is more on the back leg. Is she unsure of the water?

Muscle Habit

As a person moves their body during a particular behaviour their muscles pull them away from a free standing state. If they hold that state for prolonged periods, over time the muscles will develop to suit that way of holding them. Eventually a person's repeated behaviours can be seen by how they hold themselves.

Their muscle development tells us how they behave. In some cases we can know a great deal about a person's character before they even speak. This is one of the clues that people pick up instinctively.

Figure 6 Muscles
(Istockphoto Inc.)

Triangulated Calibration

The way you hold yourself and move about is a physical expression of your individuality and your personality. From your posture, stance and gait, your friends can recognize you from afar or quite often even in the dark, even if they are unable to see your face.' (Vijai P Sharma, PhD).

Take a look at the outline of a person standing and compare it to someone standing naturally. You will easily notice how their attitudes, emotions, culture, situation show as differences from this image.

Scanner is based on triangulated calibration, the task of setting the norms for an individual or group and assessing what this means first in comparison to universal norms and then in terms of any deviation the individual or group makes from the norm and their own established norms.

A 'norm' in this context means the usual: behaviour / belief / attitudes / commitments / paradigms / capabilities / relationships / speeds etc. When we notice the same reaction at different times, we can start to ask what do all those occasions have in common. This means we are able to be more confident about the real meaning of the observed behaviour. I am sure you would like someone to say a shift to the left means an emotional response in everyone, and although many body language speakers will suggest this is possible, that is about the art of people reading , not the science. For many situations we have to know our evidence is tested and specific to that person.

Before We Meet

Scanning often begins before we meet someone, by asking questions of ourselves that will root out our prejudices.

What is the Context of the Meeting?

1   Are you, your group or they in a position of authority or need?

2   Is there an imbalance of power - do either of you need the co-operation of the other more?

3   What are the power structures, positions of authority, knowledge etc? (see Power Plays chapter 5)

4   What other factors are in play? For example -
    · History of relationships
    · Personal data: Age/Sex/Ethnicity/Culture/Wealth/Intelligence
    · Educational differences
    · Timing perceptions of urgency
    · Time/Energy available
    · Dress codes
    · Venue issues (your place or mine), public or private
    · Comfort in these surroundings/with these people
    · Knowledge possessed by both sides
    · Support and understanding of colleagues present

Before we even meet the person we can start to construct hypotheses, to understand what we had already expected. Then we can set aside any prejudgements that are based on flimsy data. **We are preparing a base from which we can compare the reality when it arrives**. Sometimes we can ask their friends/colleagues/ managers about them if that will not affect their expectations of you or your people. Asking their competitors may also give you some insight and both sets of information need to be evaluated as opinion; not facts.

This preparedness to reject our hypotheses in the light of real data is essential to accuracy. It takes practise, see 'The Brick' exercise at the end of the book and after section 5 Professionals on the other side as an example.

Scanner is a set of tools and detailed observation processes that help us to predict what others need.

More "Before We Meet"
Other observation can begin before we meet by thinking about their:

1 Position of authority or need
2 Power structures
3 History
4 Personal data
5 Timing, context
6 Comfort
7 Knowledge
8 Support

We also need to be aware of our prejudgements and those of others.
Much of what we do in preparation is about NOT prejudging; having discovered our prejudices we need to quickly 'factor them out', to abandon their influence but not ignore that we have them and especially to be ready to abandon a judgement when the situation and the person proves it to be false.

Be prepared. Baden Powell

This is vital. If you pretend you have no prejudgement, as some extremist would have us think, you WILL be caught out. If you convince yourself you are right without sound evidence, you will most certainly be wrong in a key place.

People often say, "My first impressions are usually right." This may be the case and it is also possible that their first impression is so hard for them to correct, to admit that they were wrong, that they only see any coincident conformations of their existing view, rejecting contrary evidence as anomalies, when dealing with the person.

Clearly we need to understand our client's needs and our authorities to act. You may need to provoke a behaviour change to get your information and anyone on your side of the conversation needs to understand something of what you are doing so that they give you support, or at least to understand enough so they don't spoil, the process. More will be explained about behaviour provocation later.

With our prejudices, readiness and perhaps our environment prepared we are ready to start scanning.

> # People do not want information, they want confirmation. John Steinbeck

2.2 Notice What You Notice

Arrival – how and when people turn up.
a. Are they late/early/punctual; do they care that they are late/early/punctual?
b. Do they arrive flustered or calm?
c. Do they walk into the middle of the group and take over or stand nervously about waiting for someone else to decide where to sit?
d. Who is looking at whom to get guidance about what to do next?
e. What does their choice of clothing tell you about their attitude to the meeting, if anything?
f. What doesn't match with their apparent attitude to other things like politeness, arrogance, patience?

There are a myriad of other things that may catch your notice and it is a great start to a session if you use those wonderful social and recognition skills that humans have as a genetic gift, to check in with yourself and ask:

1 "Why did I notice that?"
2 "Does it mean anything useful?"

We use **"Notice what you notice"** frequently as a reminder while scanning. If your social, associative brain brings something to your attention, it is important to ask yourself "What is relevant about the fact that I noticed that?"

2.3 Rapport

To help in noticing, a Scanner can usefully study techniques of Rapport and I refer you to NLP for a complete description of this (Bandler & Grinder, Sue Knight, Genie Labordie, John Seymour).

Briefly - become the person you are trying to know, stand, walk and imagine speaking at their speed with their intonation, using their emphasis. Some small movement or change in breathing often tips us off about their state of mind. Try not to be obvious; they may think you are 'taking the Mickey'.

Many of us will work around a group connecting with them by imagining how we would feel if we – whatever we notice about them, e.g, stand, sit, smile, walk, etc that way. When the skills of connection become easier we notice that we can connect with more and more people, faster.

2.4 Leaders, Influencers

Who speaks first is likely to tell you both a lot about the hierarchy and the tone of the meeting.

a. Is it the leader or is someone else distracting the group for the leader?
b. Is the first statement a confrontational, placatory / polite one?
c. How is everyone sitting – forward and energetic or laid back and easy?
d. Who is mismatching in the group, who stands out as different?

As things progress and if the relationships become clearer:

e. Who defers to whom on what kind of subject?
f. Who is structured vs artistic, mature vs silly, excitable vs calm, etc?

It is not always the decision maker who is calm, deferred to, mature, etc. The way to know who is the real decision maker, is to watch at whom they look at the end of assertions and who does not look at anyone else for authority.

If you are finding it difficult to work out the decision maker, see if you can create a moment of 'unexpected doubt'. E.g, "No the contract date is not set", "We had a meeting with James" (implying that James is one of their people when in fact he is one of yours or an independent). In seeking to access their behaviour we can distract their conscious controls briefly. This is also a way to spot deception.

There is likely to be a brief moment when some of the audience look to the decision maker in order to know how to proceed. Clearly this interrupt has to be in context and a little confusing. We are playing on the common situation where someone is briefed to play the decision maker by the decision maker, and they feel slightly at risk because there is always a doubt that they may not have been told everything. They will react instinctively towards the originator. Watch them closely, they may be aware of the reaction and usually not quick enough to prevent:

1.   Averting their eyes from the decision maker
2.   Turning shoulders but not head towards them
3.   Actually looking towards them
4.   In extreme circumstances they make look for reassurance towards them and wait for permission to continue – what a give-away.

2.5 Professionals on the Other Side, (Kines, Interrupts)

Many professionals have learned to hide their thoughts and their preferred style very well, but they can't hide from Scanning if we do our job well.

To test for their real beliefs, models, commitments etc, you may need to use a cognitive and or emotional interrupt; (in Neuro Linguistic Programming they call this "Pattern Interrupt"). It can be almost anything that interrupts their state of mind and/or concentration.

Here is an example of a conversation I witnessed with a skilled Scanner intentionally presenting an **unsophisticated interrupt**.

Scenario 1 Joint Venture
(Unsophisticated Interrupts)

A skilled student Scanner used a cognitive interrupt to get some peace during a break. One member of a noisy group was about to take a chair from next to our student who asked "Can you hear the flutes?". The whole group stopped to listen for it and the volume never quite returned to the same level after that.

C1 is the CEO of the Scanner's client, **C2** is the other company's CEO and **S** is the Scanner. Coffee had been put on table a few minutes before but the conversation had been quite intense and no-one had yet taken their cup.

C1 "Thank you, I am clear now on the financials. Now we need to understand the effort needed by both sides."

C2 sat back like a 'fat cat' and seemed very pleased with himself and confident, he was smiling a broad smile. "Yes you're right, it's been useful and we will be expecting a great deal of effort from all your people; obviously you know more about this area than my people. So we want a lot of effort from you personally as well." He put his hand on C1's arm in a friendly manner.

S "Will you want sugar with that?" S was not looking at the cups but coldly staring C2 in the eyes.

C2 seemed a little fazed, he clearly expected everyone to be quiet while C1 replied and there was a brief sign of annoyance. He recovered in less than a second and said, "With the effort or the coffee?"

People smiled nervously and S looked at him coldly saying, "With the coffee."

S was able to pick up the whole of the room's structure in that second; some sat forward to stop C2 from exploding, as was clearly his way, in his own environment. C2 had betrayed his smiling façade with a moment's impatience. C1 had time to see this and to make a decision about how to respond. Obviously C1 could only do this because he was used to S's techniques.

CI "Before we go too far down that road, though, we need to understand who will be responsible for running this project on a day to day basis. They will set the management style and ethos. I am clear that these are key to the success of this project and they must be sound."

CI had made an excellent tactical change and it was clear that this was a key issue for C2 as well. His demeanour faltered and he appeared nervous, he was much less relaxed and leaned forward for the whole of the rest of the meeting.

Because of the interrupt in the usual processes, the group had to realign themselves, to recover and in those seconds they were accessing their relationships to each other; they were checking out their memories around power, history, other relationships, feelings, predictions of outcomes etc.

S was then able to help CI to grasp that C2's culture was hierarchical and not currently successful, that he was making successes by hiring good people and they were succeeding despite C2's style. CI decided to address this head on and a successful project was started that day by having one of CI's carefully selected, tough, intelligent people, who had CI's complete trust and autonomy, and one of C2's people running the project together. C2 found he had little to do; the project seemed to run itself.

Kines: Before going into Scenario 2 I want to introduce an idea described by Birdwhistell (1970) called a Kine.

Kines are such tiny specific, discrete elements of body language that the act of trying to build anything of meaning in the middle of complex interactions can be so distracting that we lose the more obvious elements of what is happening.

Birdwhistell's book is very detailed and not easy to assimilate although it is excellently observed material. An example of a Kine would be an inflection in the voice, a twitch of the face or eye. As you will see noticing a Kine was useful in Scenario 2.

A Kine is a tiny specific, discreet movement or verbal emphasis. Kines combine into more complex body language and create a picture of the person's behavioural style.

Scenario 2 Take-over

We are looking for what things occur together, behaviours and ideas that occur at the same time, or sets/sequences of behaviours that repeatedly occur.

Using the same letters C1 and S for the client and Scanner and C2 for the CEO of the other side.

This was a half a million pound company take-over; the principle components are the same for larger events. The action is condensed to the essential elements. C1 is the negotiator for the company taking over – the buyer and C2 is the negotiator for the company being taken over – the seller.

On the table were several issues: Half a million was asked for the company and goodwill, plus 200,000 for salary and holiday commitments. Another component being negotiated was the actual date of the take-over. It turned out that this was crucial to avoid a pay day that the seller would find hard to cover.

The seller wanted a decision and completion within a week. The buyer wanted the seller to believe that they would decide to buy after three weeks; although it was not necessary for them to hold out for it.

The final settlement was: 250,000 for the company and goodwill, zero salary commitments and 5,000 for holiday commitments, transfer of ownership in three weeks.

The buyers felt they got a great deal and that the Scanner helped to broker a more feasible and fair deal.

Sequence:
There was considerable fencing: accountants were in opposition; each would put a case, it would be countered and an alternative view put. This continued for some time.

The Scanner opened up the conversation to get more contribution from others on other subjects. Then the Scanner was able to reduce stance taking by using feedback, slowing explanations and giving space to speak to each person present.

A rapport was built and many general principles agreed, but there was a sticking point on the half million value. Until:

C2 "I am quite at risk, I hope you understand." Then as an aside, in a quieter voice he said, "AND my wife says I am too stressed."

As C2 said this he touched his ankle. Later in the conversation during a coffee break C2 was discussing his family who apparently were well connected with several powerful people.

S made a point of calibrating (watching all the movements, body language and verbal signals around C2 as he spoke about his family) his Kines. As he spoke about some of his family there was a distinct deference in his voice and again he reached, almost imperceptibly, for his ankle, even when the action looked really awkward.

Before the meeting reconvened, the Scanner told C1 to push the settlement figure and ask at the same time what C2 really needed. When this happened C2 grabbed his ankle in a vice-like grip and spoke with perceptible fear in his voice, saying he had put a lot of his own money into the company.

When the group broke for individual company briefing – S told C1 that C2 needed to save face with his wife, some of the money invested was clearly his wife's family's, and that he had noticed a subtle movement towards the ankle when his PA was mentioned, indicating some responsible issues. It was decided to present C2 with a deal that would enable him to continue with the new company, with his PA, and to have his investment retained in the company as shares. It was explained that he was seen as a valuable leader with a great deal of knowledge and he would be a significant director of the new company. C2 accepted the post and the significantly reduced payments. In effect, the incoming company only paid out a few thousand pounds at that point.

- What **changes and ideas** seem to occur together?
- What sets of **behaviours** do they display **repeatedly**?
- What do they do as they talk about **certain subjects**?
- What changes while they are **distracted**?

DEAD BRICK

When we teach this calibration skill we start with an exercise around a concept called 'Dead Brick'. The point of the exercise is to be aware of, and minimise, our own reactions, so that we can be more confident that what we are observing is coming from the client and not some 'hang up' of our own.

Developing 'The Brick' has additional benefits for group handling. It is an active, as opposed to passive, meditative technique: it provides access to a significantly more powerful sense/analysis/plan system that enables the practitioner to handle quite large groups with confidence and ease.

How? See exercises at the end of the book 'The Brick' and practice it.

2.6 Scanning Process Structure
Stages of Analysis

1 Create a zero space.

This needs training; there is a sequence of exercises at the end of the book including 'Watch, Eyes and Brick' (more in Book 2). It means that you will be able to pick up what is going on **with** interpretation and **without** too much prejudice. A combination of scientific observation and accessing schemas and archetypes that will be discussed later.

2 "What might it mean?"

For each piece of information/behaviour you notice, ask: "What might it mean, what evidence supports that, what else might it mean?"

3 Add to the evidence

Carry the meaning forward as a hypothesis of what is happening.

4 Continually test and retest the whole set of hypotheses as more evidence emerges.

5 Make tentative decisions, be ready to abandon them.

6 Test these by 'cognitive' interrupts (challenges to what the client expects) and simple questions.

a. Cognitive interrupts can be anything eg,

"You seem unsure."

"Is blue higher than red was yesterday or is that tomorrow?"

An apparently no-sense sentence that causes a pause.

b. **Simple questions:**

"Is it always the case that...?"

"So what is your ideal?"

"How much does that annoy you?"

"What part of ...are we discussing?"

> The point at which to interrupt is a key, experienced-based decision and the effective Scanner will need a great deal of knowledge about personality types, psychological personality theory, archetypes (See Chapter 6 Style, Typologies section iii Archetypes) and exemplars to choose the appropriate interrupt.
>
> 7 **Create a series of whole person hypotheses** until you have a model of the person. This model is then the basis of interpretation and can be re-written based on future evidence.

Fairly quickly you will find you are no longer guessing, you have evidence.

Certainty comes from understanding the causes and structures of behaviour; the next chapter will give the reader a good grounding in those.

I have found out that there ain't no surer way to find out whether you like people or hate them than to travel with them.

MARK TWAIN

HUMAN CODE

Chapter 3

HUMAN CODE

How can we be sure what we see is usable?

PURPOSE:

To introduce the physical building blocks of behaviour, so that the reader can work from the source, create their own techniques and use these with more skill and depth of expertise.

OUTCOMES

On completion of this chapter the reader will be able to:

1 Describe how behaviours, knowledge and skills are coded and modified in the brain
2 Describe Signal anxiety
3 Describe a schema
4 Explain how emotion can override thinking

METHOD

A description is given of the building blocks of memory, and the storage of experience and reaction in the brain.

May your head protect you where your heart takes you and never the other way around.

Cliff Edwards

It seems that many who use their Brain before their hearts end up being sad. Those who use their heart before their brain are often poor; while those who balance the two seem to be the happiest.

How can we be sure what we see is usable?

3.1 Encoding

It is clear that the real motivation of people can be an apparent chaotic thing. So how can we call it a science?

The mind is very complex, yet emerged from a simple binary logic, 'yes or no', neurons fire or do not fire. We know this because we have opened up brains and looked at their working units; neurons. Have a look at the next illustration.

2003 Focus Education Australia

Figure 7 Neuron

Image used with kind permission from John Joseph, Focus Education Australia.

They pass on a charge to other neurons based on a decision – shall I discharge? (we might call this a one) or shall I not discharge? (we can call this a zero). The more often it fires the more readily it fires and this means that as we think, some routes through our brain become preferred – learning occurs, habits and thought relationships are created.

THEORY – NEUROLOGY

If you like theory and the 'nuts and bolts' you may be interested in the basic logic of decision making in neurology which I have put in Appendix 2 'Decision making Neurons'.

Q How can we be sure what we are seeing is significant?
A We are looking for what is repeated, coded, behavioural patterns. These are neurologically coded actions.

Q And in English?
A Some things people do, they can change easily, others are written, almost wired into the brain by genetics and experience.

Q Can you make it even simpler?
A Some things you can change, other things are harder to change so people find it hard to hide those reactions.

SO WHAT?

If everything in the brain is coded in this way it seems clear that every time a particular stimulus occurred then we would react in exactly the same way. To an extent this is true and as a Scanner it is very useful to be able to reproduce the same or similar action in a person. It enables us to calibrate, to work out what ideas and words are linked in a person. By repeating a set of words in isolation, watching how the person reacts we can isolate which ideas mean what to the person.

Example 1 Timing – Rhythms (Cross Modal)

Imagine our client is tapping their thumb in a certain beat, say 2,1 time (two fast beats, a pause and a single beat), while they are apparently intentionally slowing down, even holding up, a process.

Minutes later as another person enters the room they sit back and tap out the same beat with their feet. This can point to: a source of reticence, agitation, any holding back or a link to show they have difficulties with the person who entered or that the person reminds them of difficulties or risk taking.

The pattern repeats because it links to similar memories which are stored in particular neuron patterns. The neurons may frequently fire in the same way, which allows us to predict the person's behaviour.

Another example: someone scratches their neck while you are asking a question and then they shift and present confidently. They make a mistake, and they scratch their neck again.

For this person scratching the neck at a particular moment adds to your confidence that they are nervous at that moment. It can also mean this is a person capable of presenting confidently, even when they are really feeling insecure.

This mechanism of repeating patterns is extremely useful but it is not the whole story. Some people, especially professionals, can change their reactions; they are actually capable of altering the way their neurons react, suppressing or diverting energy. Indeed, we can teach people to cover their reactions for short periods.

HOW?

1 By engaging other neurons (the client uses a concept in their mind to divert the reaction) eg, "I want to be unhelpful or to shout at you but I would be punished for doing so. I am a professional, watch just how professional I can be (not emotionally engaged)."

2 Chemically -
   a. Artificial drugs eg, alcohol
   b. Hormones eg, adrenaline, cortisol, testosterone (although the action of testosterone may not be as clear as we once thought)

3 Tiredness/alertness can suppress or support neuron transmissions.

4 Context - if the person perceives the situation differently their neurons will react differently.

5 Recent events, local effects (a smile or frown from someone).

Example 1b How Reactions can be Changed
So signals may change over the course of an interview, particularly if they are prolonged or over a meal.

The environment can also change reactions, heightened sensitivities, e.g, an unsympathetic boss enters the conversation, or being at home with family around as opposed to being in an office in a possibly competitive situation.

PROVE IT
We have a habit of looking in one direction when thinking about the future and another when thinking about the past (NLP, Bandler & Grinder). Try this simple exercise; it works most of the time. Ask someone to describe the past and then the future in some detail including any colours, sounds etc. It is possible to work out where their eyes look as they think about past or future and usually these are different directions. If the person looks to their left to think about the future and right for the past, when we ask them to keep looking left and describe the past in some detail they will find the urge to look to the right very powerful.

Now, if you are asked about a holiday and you usually look up and to the left, by thinking instead about a conversation you will have tomorrow with a travel agent about a future holiday, you may start to look down to the right.

SO WHAT?

This is an indication of two very useful things:

1 Patterns of Neurology

Behaviours and actions that go together in a particular person can be very strongly ingrained or encoded behaviours and extremely difficult to temporarily falsify, so this can be useful as a lie detector. For example, in interviews, a person assuring the interviewer that they have a certain experience but who continually looks to their future (each person may differ in where they look for past and future) may in fact be imagining what to say to pretend they have done it. This is only an indication that there may be an issue, not hard evidence. For instance, they may have done the job frequently and be thinking about how they may change it in the future. You will need to watch closely for their initial reactions.

2 Spatial Coding

Figure 8 Car Crash – Encoded Action

It seems that many ideas and memories are stored in the brain and accessed in some way that mimics the structure of the outside world. For example, if someone saw a car crash, even though they are now in an office nowhere near the crash, they will show the path the car took with their hands and you can see their eyes following the action. When people describe their home verbally and mentally walk through it, one can see their eyes following passages and turns as if they were actually doing it. Occasionally, if you ask someone to think of a time of day, you can guess of what time they are thinking by watching their eye movements. This is not foolproof, and it suggests that some of us at least store information spatially.

If things are ordered in the brain in a spatial way then we ought to be able to observe people playing out, pointing, and gesticulating as if they were actually in the place that their imaginations are creating. In fact this is so. A Scanner can often tell when a problem occurred, if the client is thinking about it in a sequence, by watching their hands or eyes while they play out what has happened. In this situation it has been possible to tell clients at what point they did something, sometimes even years ago, and sometimes when they had not remembered consciously on their own.

These observable patterns can be used to help us to understand the relevance, relationships and priorities of issues in our clients. Here is a little more theory around how coding might be happening.

3.2 Sources of Coding

Encoding is the process of setting up a group of memory cells (neurons) to represent something, a memory, an action, a belief, an analytical process. We can often observe how a person analyses an idea or confrontation and we can notice to what each idea is linked and how they sort information. It then becomes easier to predict how they will react. If we question one person's skills, they may be happy to discuss it, while if we question their intent, they feel that is out of bounds. Equally another person may be completely the other way around. The way we decide, in this case - to be offended or not, can be complex and hard for the novice to understand. Once we take time to isolate the elements of offence it becomes a lot easier to predict.

A common example is the manger/leader who will welcome criticism in private but react violently to the smallest doubt in public.

There will be a set of acceptable behaviours 'in public' and 'in private' for our example. The more a thing is conceptually close to another, the stronger the link. This may be one of the reasons that free association and 'slips of the tongue' work in psychoanalysis.

It seems that we put things, ideas, information, in sets of relationships **CONTEXTS** so that they build a network of interconnected relationships.

Word Association

Word association is described well in the literature and is reproduced very simply here, for illustration only. The analyst reads a list of words and for each the client says the first word that occurs to them. The analyst is waiting to hear anything out of place, a change in response speed, an unusual link of words. This might point to a model the patient has that in turn produced unexpected behaviour.

ANALYST	CLIENT
BLACK	WHITE
UP	DOWN
MOTHER	FATHER
CAT	DOG
WALK	DRAG
RUN	WALK
SLOW	HARD
FAST	SLOW

Table I Simple Word Association

The responses are fairly common until 'Walk'. The analyst decides that the response 'Drag' is unusual enough to test the link and responds with the word they expected. They do this to try to understand how the patient links Walk and Drag. The analyst says 'Run' and gets back the usually paired word 'Walk', which he used before. Again the usual response to Slow is Fast and the analyst tries the same converse link and finds a one-way relationship that causes the expected response to be sublimated (replaced by a word with a stronger association, the effect of this is that the original word is covered, pushed down in a metaphorical list of choices of response) and an alternative used.

3.3 Using the Code

This might lead the analyst to discuss time pressures in the client's life. However, for business, when we notice someone not using an obvious word in preference for a more flamboyant or less flamboyant word, we can start to think about what might be causing the choice change in our client; do they try to impress, are they using words inappropriately to manipulate the outcomes.

We may find there is a definite avoidance of certain words or ideas. When an idea is closely linked with another in someone, by causing them to think about the first idea, they will sense the other's presence even before they think about the other directly. This is how something called 'signal anxiety' operates. See Appendix 3.

SO WHAT?

When we work with a client we can test a theory, e.g, that their fear of someone is clouding an issue. We do this by saying the name and watching the reaction in the instant we say it. Do they access behaviour that we know they display when they are anxious, does their eye accessing freeze, etc?

Signal Anxiety

The theory of signal anxiety suggests that particular ideas or memories have links to emotions like fear and that the pathways towards this painful memory also start to link with pain. We get used to the pain arising every time we think near that memory so even the paths leading to the memory start to be linked with pain. As these associations strengthen, the brain will begin to redirect the person's thoughts before they reach the original or causative memory. In effect this means that a painful memory is suppressed. We no longer remember why we are afraid of say, yellow, because the event that caused the fear can no longer be accessed without also accessing associated painful thoughts in advance.

If we were constantly aware of embarrassing moments or things that cause us fear, the everyday process of getting through the day would be very difficult. Some argue that this is the primary purpose of an 'unconscious' part of our mind. Others argue there is no unconscious mind. However, there seems to be an inbuilt pain avoidance process.

Emotion - Amygdale

The neurons near a memory that was accessed in association with an emotion will recreate emotions when accessed again – the brain is an associating machine and it will stimulate an organ deep in the brain called the amygdale. Among other processes, the amygdale will send hormone signals out and some of these access other parts of the brain making a person ready to fight or run, and it can operate faster than the person can think. It means we can react to a threat before we consciously understand it is there.

The brain is an associating machine.

Associations are built in this way (Skinner, 1976). As other networks of neurons access the area of such an emotional memory, they also begin to be associated with the memory and the association spreads out around the memory, getting less powerful as it spreads further from the origin. It is like a drop of ink on a wet paper towel, as the ink spreads out it gets thinner. Or like the spread of a fungus on a Petri dish. Even at the outer reaches of the influence the person may start to sense there is something discomforting associated with their current thought. This is signal anxiety and it is very helpful to understand it and to notice it.

SO WHAT?

Watching our client we may notice anxiety flick across their face as a certain area is discussed. As the conversation continues we can build a picture of where, in their thinking processes, are their real anxieties. Knowing the real source of anxiety in key members of a group helps us to understand where conflict and confusion is 'stuck' and so it helps us intervene and clear away the confusion in: the group psyche, any processes or tasks. "Group think" or cultural fables form a mass of seemingly impenetrable barriers to reconciliation, I presented a paper on this issue in Kenya in 2005 with Paul McCarthy. We have found linguistic structures that clear this fog and may develop a book in the future to share these.

What is 'Group Psyche'? This is a way of understanding the overall personality of a group, as if they formed one person with whom you are communicating.

I believe **Freud** felt that **'culture' could be described as group psychosis.** When I first heard this I laughed out loud in a presentation as I recognised the power of this simple idea, even if it is only partly true it is very useful.

HOW

Do we intervene? Some Scanners utilise methods derived from provocative coaching. This is a method based on elements of Provocative Therapy by Frank Farralley (1989).

If the reader is interested in Provocative coaching they may want to contact 'The Centre for Provocative coaching' www.realise.org/pc. Provocative coaching has been characterised as a cheeky, insightful and warm-hearted approach to serious issues that causes a sharing of insight. For the UK Provocative therapy group contact Phil Jeremia www.provocativetherapy.co.uk.

Alternatively we use the idea of Charged words. When we notice a concern around certain words we can test the word. Here is an example of how the conversation might go:

Example 2 Words of Special Relevance
(Complex Equivalents and Charged Words)

The Scanner now knows that the source of tension is around the person's view of work as a thing, separate from themselves in some way. This is a choice of that working style and a belief system that needs to be respected as neither right nor wrong. If the person had reacted differently it may have shown a lack of differentiation 'I am what I do' approach.

It is vital to remember that no one isolated piece of evidence can be taken as fact, it needs to be tested and considered in a wider context. By isolating this tiny part of a conversation here, I may have given too much weight to its significance. A Scanner is always referring evidence to the context to find relevance.

By using provocative coaching we can go further, deeper although it may become extremely confrontational. At this level only an experienced provocative coach would continue; new Scanners would reduce the conflict at this point and use other processes.

C=Client **S**=Scanner

C "It has been some time since we have been able to close the quarterly accounts on time."

S "What has been the problem?"

C (Slight jerk in demeanour)   "No problem, it is just that we had problems with a change over of accounts staff last year and we are still clearing up the outstanding queries."

Now on the face of it this person is contradicting themselves; "there is no problem we just had problems…" This is not uncommon; they have two meanings for the same word. "You have a problem" is a criticism. "There were problems" is a process. When the Scanner starts again he changes the subject for a few sentences and then re-approaches the word again.

S "So your problem with the process is that it takes time to reconcile and delays things."(Here the Scanner is trying to find out if the two words "Your problem" are isolated in the client's mind or will he place the context around process as the rest of his sentence is focussed – "…it takes time…")

C (The client shows the same jerk in behaviour indicating that the positioning of "your" and "problem" have real significance. This is confirmed by the emotional reaction.) "No (pause) I don't have a problem with it, it is just something we have to deal with."

S "I understand it is not caused by you and there are problems you have to deal with. Thank you, I am glad that we are clear on that."

3.4 People Programmes (Schema)
"Reading the structure of individuals' thinking"

This section is very theoretical and it is arguable whether it should be in a practical book. However, it is worthwhile persevering through the theory of the structure of thinking so that you can create scanning tools for yourself.

Schema and Schema Programmes

Schema

The term Schema was first used in a similar way by Jean Piaget in 1926. Gick and Holyoak, 1983, describe schema as "...a description of the essence of something".

Schema n. A plan, diagram, or outline, especially a mental representation of some aspect of experience, based on prior experience and memory, structured in such a way as to facilitate (and sometimes to distort) perception, recognition, the drawing of inferences or the interpretation of new information in terms of existing knowledge.
Oxford Dictionary of Psychology 2003.

The resultant effect is a set of programmes with which we interpret the world and make decisions. As Paul Watzlawick explains (Watzlawick 1993, p.119):

"...We never deal with reality per se, but rather with images of reality - that is, with interpretations. While the number of potentially possible interpretations is very large, our world image usually permits us to see only one - and this one therefore appears to be the only possible, reasonable, and permitted view. Furthermore, this one interpretation also suggests only one possible, reasonable, and permitted solution, and if we don't succeed at first we try and try again - or, in other words, we resort to the recipe of doing more of the same."

Watzlawick

Schema Programmes

A schema programme is a sequence of linked concepts. Schemas link together in relationships that model our expectations of the world, of actions and reactions. See Appendix 3, "Spreading Activation" for a technical description of how this might work neurologically". Some might say that they don't just represent the world, for the individual they ARE the world. So much so that evidence from the world that contradicts these programmes may be discarded in preference for the model. The assertion is that the belief is so inflexibly held that no evidence can change it. I believe people can choose; if they know they are choosing. See the section on Giraffes Chapter 6 Style/Typologies, part 2 Maturity. So let's spend some time understanding these Schemas and Schema programmes, perhaps perversely the programmes first.

Schema Programme Contraction

Schema contractions provide a means to short-cut thinking which has been essential for us to survive physically: in terms of danger avoidance, food finding and for social interaction. In the everyday complex interactions we need to function with a semblance of continuity.

For Example:

1. When it rains the river floods, the ox gets stuck, I can catch the ox, we will eat.

2. When He frowns, His reactions may be unpredictable, that leads to problems, we will argue.

So raining means food and frowns mean arguments.
The structure of a thought construction:

Occurrence A often occurs with event B
Event B usually/often/always causes C
Experience suggests that:
the eventual outcome of C is D
Therefore I can expect A to lead to D

Example 3 Refining Schema Programmes

> **A** Jim arrives and **B** he **always** asks awkward questions.
> which **always** means **C** I will not be able to answer the questions.
> **C = D** I will feel foolish and then angry.

The schema programme 'Jim arrives' ends with 'I will be angry'. So the whole Schema programme has been contracted. If this contracted form runs enough times, the original process may even be extinguished from memory, the client would forget it was about Jim's questions and his feeling of foolishness. Jim makes him angry. Eventually people similar to Jim will make him angry. (See 'Signal Anxiety.')

Resolution

By changing the programme, making it more specific as in: 'Jim arrives at work' we can add a neural interrupt into the process. In practice people often find meeting outside of work can generate this kind of differentiation in expectation; they seem to be able to start again simply by staying away from work issues until trust is built.

Whether we do it or they do, it generates an 'IF' in the middle of the sequence so it becomes: A – B Jim arrives and IF it is at work THEN he will ask awkward questions, **OTHERWISE** he may not. This has generated a new 'Jim arrives' programme with the sequence 'He may not ask awkward questions and we will get useful things done'.

When we meet new situations we search for existing programmes to help us to know how to be prepared and deal with the new situation. The benefit of this kind of 'optioning' is in providing us with more flexibility in our expectations otherwise we will tend to overuse inappropriate programmes. A question for the reader: is it possible that we could all get on famously with each other if our schemas were completely flexible? What are the dangers of being that flexible?

Example 4 Generalisation of Schema Programme

The thought 'Jim arrives' can be generalised to 'X arrives'. X can then mean anyone. When we have an 'IF' in the programme somewhere as in the above example 'IF it is at work,' then the client will wait for more evidence before becoming fearful. Remember that signal anxiety means they will start to sense some fear already even though it may not be Jim as the subject of the programme. It is worth noting here that bits of a programme can be shared with other programmes. (See Illustration of Schema Programme.)

The brain is very effective at storage and utilisation of programmes. So in the middle of a conversation a concept may arise that causes the person to access a section of memory that links to emotion, mistrust, fear, longing etc, that changes the nature of their relationship to the conversation, often in ways that cause the other person to wonder what happened.

Extants

When there are lots of sub programmes running the individual may become confused, worried and nervous, even angry. The number of places in the brain that 'extants' (unfinished thoughts) can be kept is limited in most of us. As these are overloaded the thinking can become chaotic, aggressive, confused. What do you do when you lose your place and you feel anxious? One has a choice that is affected by maturity of communication style. Some will admit their confusion and set about getting clarity, others will cover up hoping to catch up later, some get annoyed as if others are intentionally confusing an issue. It is interesting to note that in Ericksonian hypnosis (Milton Erickson in Rosen 1991) advantage is taken of incomplete ideas to create a trance state. (see also Personality this chapter).

Causality Fading and Choice Point

The intervening steps between 'Jim arrives' and 'I will be angry' will fade in terms of excitation if the sequence occurs often enough. Eventually the neural route from 'Jim arrives' to 'I will be angry' that went through C and D is replaced by the brain to provide a faster route. The original links fade so the new route takes over and the person is less troubled by having to make a choice and by the additional, 'unnecessary' thinking required to get from A to D. The Choice point, that is the decision about which route to take, will be changed so strongly that the intervening reasons are cut out of the process. There will still be some activity along the original route, otherwise we could never recall it and evidence of working with people over the years suggests we can almost always recover memories. If we are to re-programme an unhelpful short cut that has been running for a while, we need to re-enliven the original, now perhaps almost inaccessible route. For an explanation of how to do this see 'Exercise Reverse Anchoring'.

Exemplars
The building blocks of programmes.

Exemplar n. An instance or representative of a concept; more generally something to be copied or imitated.
Oxford Dictionary of Psychology 2003.

It seems that humans develop mental representations, exemplars as described by Roth (1995) p34. She demonstrates how a series of exposures to examples of a thing or concept produces a typicality effect. These are a set of parameters that allow the person to categorise things and concepts. For example a person may have a set of rules that an object is a cup and not a bowl because of the relative size of the handle to the bowl and the flatness of the bowl. These exemplars become ever more refined as we see more and more examples.

A schema is similar and more active; it attaches sets of behaviours and or reactions to situations / specific stimuli. Jaqueline Sachs, Sachs et al., (1985) describes a system of **"Scripts"** that might be thought of as the emergent effect of these exemplars and schemas.

So the brain seems to store memories in relationship with each other. I will give an overview of how it organises ideas starting with the small units of related concepts working up to complex linked ideas.

Detailed Memories

Some memories can be quite detailed; in vivid dreams we can recall clear images.

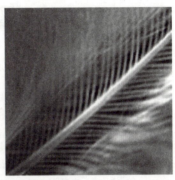

Figure 9 Storage of Detail in Memory

Clearly this is inefficient in terms of storage and when someone is recalling an image rather than an emotionally related series of ideas, a **schema sequence**, it is possible to notice a pause and often the eyes will move as if accessing the memory in the world outside the brain; see 'eye accessing'.

Exemplars Detail

We construct basic descriptions of discrete objects, feelings and simple events. We store these efficiently as minimal descriptions - exemplars. E.g, a cup exemplar might be made up of only those concepts that are necessary for a thing to be a cup. For each of us that may be slightly different. For me it has to hold something that would empty out if the prevailing force changed relative direction, ie gravity. It also has a depth that causes me to differentiate it from a bowl or a saucer.

If it has a handle, then that increases the likelihood that it is a cup. So a shallow cup with no handle might also be called a soup bowl.

Figure 10 Exemplar

The exemplar is the prototype, a model of how something is or how something acts. It is a minimalist description of something, it stores the essence of a thing as efficiently as possible, so that we can recognise the thing even if it changes some of its size, shape, colour etc.

In this way we construct a 'tool box' of concepts and objects that we can reconstruct in many ways to reconstruct larger concepts and objects in our memory. This idea is supported by research into "Cliques" (Tsien 2000), these are groups of neurons that act together to create the perception of a concept.

In the same way, and from infancy on, we piece together how the world acts and reacts to us in chains of smaller concepts to make larger, more complex concepts. We formulate theories or beliefs about what the world is likely to do in various situations. These expectations become linked and interrelated in ever more complex ways and become sequences or programmes I have called schema programmes.

Basic schemas are constructed by linking the exemplars, the very simple basic objects, with relationships. This produces chains of ideas.

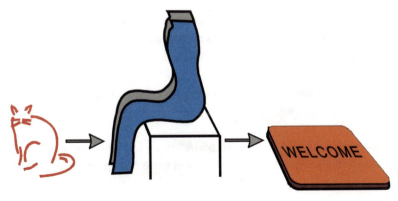

Figure 11 Exemplars - Schemas

Here is a set of exemplars and links forming a schema that most English speaking children learn to read in their first reader.

"The Cat Sat on the Mat".

If we added to this an instruction about what to do when the cat sat on the mat it would form a Schema programme. So, "When the Cat sits on the mat it wants to be fed so it will purr until I feed it, so I should go to the cupboard and get its food."

We can compare the relationship between exemplars and schemas to a string of pearls where the pearls are the exemplars and the string linking each pearl to the next is the relationship between each exemplar. The whole pearl necklace is the schema. The associations around the necklace in time, when to wear it, where to find it, how to pick it up, put it around a neck and fix it, who else might be involved, would be the Schema programme.

Objects/Sub-Routines

Each element above is as simple as I could make it and the links are simple one to one connections. However, real programmes can be far more complex than a simple straight line. A way to represent the whole programme would be a three dimensional spider's web, showing ideas connected to several other ideas. Sometimes thoughts will trigger other thoughts and the resulting thought is a mixture of parts of schemas, commonly used "Sub-routines" (or Object in computer programming jargon.)

E.g, "I am not good - at mathematics - so when problems - are presented - I will feel uneasy - leading to panic - **I deal badly** with **panic** - and it will be clear that my mathematics is poor - I will be ridiculed, - feel rejected - and invalid."

At another time: "I don't know - these people - if I panic - (**I deal badly with panic**) - I will look scared."

The **sub-routine "I deal badly with panic"** is used by both programmes. In computing a routine that can be used as part of more than one programme is called a Polymorph.

These sub-routines are the objects scanners use and study most often. By understanding critical sub-routines in our client's and subject's thinking and how they link to behaviour we can predict behaviour better. We can also elicit behaviour by causing our client to access a particular sub-routine to get a state of mind that we need in a negotiation or reconciliation.

If we are concerned to have a person explain carefully we might continue to use their title with an embedded form as in example 5 below.

Example 5 Embedded Form – Accessing Useful Self Images

The enboldened words are spoken very slightly slower or with more emphasis to focus the attention on the word.

"Tell me, **professor**, how can you **contrast** the two **options?**".

I first cause the subject to mentally access their academic memory, reinforce that with a word from their undergraduate days.

I then contrast, and reinforce the idea of logic rather than emotion with the word options rather than choices. If instead I used the following, I might get a more emotionally based response.

"Why do you do it that way?"

Firing off the desired schemas is about observation and calibration, (see Calibration). So schemas are linked ideas and schema programmes are constructions of thoughts utilising keyed elements of schemas.

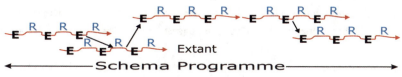

Figure 12 Schema Programme Structure (String of Pearls)

A Schema links ideas/relationships and Exemplars.
Clearly I have used a simple example. Other concepts such as "I like", "I admire" and "I enjoy" are differentiated in similar ways. When we link all these programmes together, we have a schema sequence, a program that goes from input (stimulus) to, often complex, output (reaction).

Extants

You may have noticed the word Extant at the end of an unfinished schema in the illustration. When energy diverts in the middle of a thought to another thought, the original thought often fades. However, if it doesn't, the person is left with a feeling of 'Unfinished business' – a distraction of the mind. How many of these a person can tolerate may indicate their level of coping, which will be a function of their intelligence, experience, organisation, functioning and tiredness. This is useful information in a negotiation.

Behaviourists like Watson, Skinner, Pavlov, Wundt might go no deeper than observable behaviour in searching for human intention. They might say that this is as complete and necessary a description of the human process as possible.

3.5 Mechanism or Mind

"To be or not to be?"

Is decision making a process of proactive choice or the resolution of chaos?

It is possible to operate as a Scanner on the behaviourist level; believing that all choice is an illusion. A pure behaviourist would assert that the brain is in a complex state of action reaction during difficult choices and that the interplay of pre-programmed behaviours result in a choice that – given sufficient access and time to the brain one could predict. This suggests we are like complex calculators.

However, Scanners can use their own social or rapport building techniques to approximate outcomes. The more effective Scanners operate on the expectation that, given a pause in these programmes the individual seems to be able to make a personal decision to change the process. This is an assertion that the Mind, as distinct from the brain, is capable of real individual choice, which further implies individuation or 'divine' capability. This apparent choice is theoretically an impossibility and as such it is proof of one of two things:

Either:
1. **We are deluded.**
2. **There is free will.**

It does not seem possible to prove which, but read René Descartes for a treatment of the issue. My interpretation of his proposal for proof that the person exists is:

"There is a pause in which thought occurs implying the existence of a Thinker which will be called I."

Usually quoted as **"I think therefore I am."**
With apologies for the approximation to the society for the appreciation of Descartes.

The existence of real choice is debatable. What one might call an example of this choice would be a person acting out of character or out of programme; apparently choosing to break their programming. I would argue that this is an example of programme differentiation; so hold more to the behaviourist's view. They are interrupting a lower level schema with a higher level schema.

As explained in Chapter 1, most of what we do is pre-programmed (Eagle & Pentland Structure in Routine (2006)). Programmes are pre-ordered in priority, e.g survival is high priority. One might suspend one's curiosity in a dangerous situation. Abraham Maslow (1945 & 1957) put our drivers into a hierarchy of needs.

Maslow:
1. Physiological: hunger, thirst, bodily imperatives
2. Safety/security: out of danger
3. Belonging (Love): affiliate with others, be accepted
4. Self Esteem: to achieve, be competent, gain approval and recognition
5. A sense of purpose
6. Self Actualisation: a process of reassessing oneself and creating considered changes

Most of what we do and think is outside our conscious intervention.

For the purpose of clarity there is little practical difference to the **outcome** of scanning whether choice is an emergent pattern from chaos or if it is divine choice. Either way it requires us to have and use patterning skills – seeing the patterns using our network thinking (mainly right brain skills), analysing them with our serial/sequential (mainly left brain skills).

ROLE SETS
Before going further, I will briefly mention a high order set of schemas called Role sets. We seem to have the ability to quickly adopt complete sets of schemas from others by observation; a sort of 'Job lot' or 'Package deal'. It is surprising how quickly and easily these complex social programmes can be acquired. Sachs et al (1985) talks about a similar idea called "Scripted events"; we seem to adopt these pre-scripted roles to suit social events. These can be very complex and may be a source of our beliefs and values.

Roles

It may be that in early life social interaction seems quite complex, even daunting. As children, as we interact, we may adopt tiny plays or "role moments", which are highly organised, well observed, personalised and developed behaviour trails – linked units of individual behaviour responses that together form a complex system that becomes a tool. More simply put, we might watch others and take on ways of acting that seem successful.

In later life we may be labelled or judged according to these sets of acts, as if they defined us.

Others may sometimes expect certain stereo typical patterns from us, by virtue of our appearance, age, sex etc. This may be an attribute of our human abilities at social interaction that give us abilities to develop quite sophisticated coping strategies. It is often important to re-evaluate these; to, as it were, open up the box of recordings and decide what we want to keep and what may be updated, changed or set aside.

As children we learn these quite complex behaviours in order to deal with situations, they become complex and inter-linked into role sets or programmes. Role sets (habituated, archetype responses) are often viewed as **being** the person, rather than their behaviour. It is vital, if we are to gain any control of our behaviour and thus to our lives that we get access to our programs and can change them if we so desire. Even before that **the first step is to recognise that they exist and that they are affectation, pasted on behaviours rather than who we are.**

How much of your behaviour has developed without conscious decision?

3.6 Emotion

Emotions can interrupt all schemas, they are driven by our original animal brain which is situated at the core of the part of our brain that developed later. See Chapter 6 Typologies figure 42 Conceptual map of the brain.

It is a very sophisticated person who can control these to the extent that we are not able to see their effect in: a blush, heart rate change, eye dilation, attention shift, posture freeze and a number of other key changes.

"Hormones are the messengers of the body. They are chemicals released under order of the brain, via electrical messages down nerves from the brain to different organs around the body. These small organs, or glands, then make and release their own specific hormones. These hormones tell other organs to make different chemicals or to control blood supply. Here's an example - when your brain wants to tell your heart to pump faster to help your muscles outrun the animal chasing you, within microseconds, the nerve impulse has told the adrenal gland to release its hormone. This hormone is adrenaline and this takes the message to the heart as well as other organs in preparation for running."

These processes have links to other parts of the brain dedicated to emotional responses. The action of the amygdale and associated neurology can produce instant self protecting activity as well as setting off hormone production all over the body, including in the brain, that can remotely change observable behaviour and the route of thoughts everywhere in the brain, causing significantly different behaviours, perceptions, thinking, feeling and outcomes.

The clearest illustration of the existence of the effect of a self, or at least ego, is the flush response to embarrassment. Useful in a tribal culture to show that an action had upset or attracted someone, this response can happen unexpectedly. For instance if a person becomes aware that they should not have lied, even if no-one else is aware of the lie. In terms of our survival it might be better for the person not to blush. The blush response means that in some way they have connected self awareness (e.g. embarrassment) to physical effect. Is this mind over matter?

Hormone Distributors

Pineal - 24hr rhythms sleep/awareness (influenced by light levels)

Hypothalamus - thirst, appetite, temperature

Pituitary - egg or sperm, testosterone, menstruation, lactation and general cell development, skin pigmentation, fluid balance

Thyroid - metabolism

Parathyroid - blood calcium levels

Thymus - production of T-lymphocyte – autoimmune system.

Adrenal - fight-flight, stress

Pancreas - digestion, growth

Ovaries/Testes - development of sexual characteristics

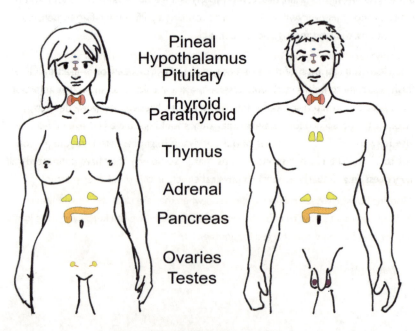

Pineal
Hypothalamus
Pituitary

Thyroid
Parathyroid

Thymus

Adrenal

Pancreas

Ovaries
Testes

Figure 13 Sites Distributing Hormonal Controls
Nick Biggs and Cliff Edwards

Many of these programmes have been written into us by thousands of years of trial and error. We are born with programmes that protect us; babies throw their arms out and back if they fall backwards. Such code is clearly very useful and clearly coded genetically; anyone without the programme who fell backwards and cracked their heads because they did not throw their arms out may have died, thus removing the humans who have the lack of that genetic material from the population. Of course we then add in more coding, as we experience our world, to become more adapted to our specific environment.

SO WHAT?

We need to add these genetic reactions to the behavioural "soup". We need to become aware of what is intentional and unintentional, what we and our clients can address/change and what they are suppressing. Then we are able to focus our energies more productively.

3.7 Incomplete Programmes

If many programmes, perhaps from different sources, genetic, behavioural, cognitive, are running in a person's mind and some are incomplete the client may become confused, lose their place and be unable to resolve their state of mind. Enough of this will cause e.g confusion or trance, (see Rosen on Erickson 1991) depending on other, simultaneous states of mind. It is important for us to notice this confusion, what we do with it will depend on what we want. It is literally fascinating.

SO WHAT?

Noticing how behaviour changes in a person when they are calm and when they are excited also tells us how to elicit the response we need – we can keep everything low key for one outcome and charged for another.

Example 6 Match - Lead

CLIENT	SCANNER
"Well I want to fix that straight away"	"When?"
"Now"	"Who's going to make it happen?"
"I am"	"You?"
"Yes me"	"Sure?"
Absolutely"	"What are you doing sitting here with me then?"
"I'm not, I'm going to go and do it now"	"When?"
GONE.....	

If a client is making rash or hurried decisions we can continually talk slowly and softly making the end of every sentence quieter and slower. Often this will cause a sympathetic slowing in their thinking.

As they calm down one can notice their decisions changing radically from high risk to conciliatory thinking (thinking that is mostly around what can I say/do, what can I give, in order to get the other to agree). This is a technique used by police, therapists, hypnotists and negotiators.

If you have seen evangelists or motivational speakers working, they sometimes create acceleration in their speech that also causes a sympathetic increase in heart rate and cognitive expectation in the audience. Listen to the music in a horror or action film, as the action increases so does the tempo of the music, often simulating the heart beat that goes with the feelings the director is trying to get the audience to feel. Try watching a scary part of a familiar fantasy film with the sound turned off, or with music designed for infants and notice how you respond differently.

As a client begins to make positive decisions and commitments the Scanner might start to use short clipped sentences to encourage their decisions and courage.

3.8 Personality - Identity

Some of our programmes are closely keyed to emotion and others may also be keyed to identity patterns, to a concept of 'This is who I am'. When this happens we feel engaged personally with the process. We may feel threatened, at risk, offended, complimented, challenged etc. The 'Cold' in our model of personality types in Chapter 6 will have lots of dampening around these links so that emotions are almost walled off. Be warned, these walls leak and feelings build underneath their apparent calmness.

Accessing the **schema of identity** in a calm state can increase a person's sense of self possession and personal identity. This often causes them to be clearer and more confident. All too often, however, the identity is only accessed in moments of crisis, elation or depression. All of which will cloud a real perception of self. We designed a process to help our clients to stimulate their access to their identity in a way that avoids barriers to clarity around humility and arrogance. They become aware of the links to their 'Who am I?' Schema and Schema programmes. People have called it **'Trial Identity'** or 'Who Are You?'.

It is a formal, structured process of careful elicitation, pulling out, unravelling ideas from their thinking, preferably using sensitive support from professionals. We ask them to think of roles they fill that they enjoy, then get them to combine these roles by first asking what outcomes they have and then what role in general covers two or more of those outcomes.

We repeat this until they conclude with an overall identity statement. We then test their commitment to that identity. If the commitment is missing we go back to the roles and test each one to be sure it is stated accurately and that it accurately represents their intentions. Readers can use the 'Trail Identity' form from our web site to run this exercise - www.realise.org/identity

> "If you can meet with triumph and disaster and treat those two impostors just the same..."
>
> "IF" Rudyard Kipling 1865 – 1936

Part 2
Applying & Using Scanner
(Observable Behaviour)

Purpose

To explain the causes and means of analysing, directly observable behaviour.

This is the simplest and most easily recognised route to understanding the intentions of others. Both these observable and inferred behaviours are needed for a complete picture and for any certainty.

This section requires active experimentation by the reader to derive experience.

Simply look with perceptive eyes at the world about you, and trust to your own reactions and convictions.

ANSEL ADAMS

BODY LANGUAGE

Chapter 4

PHYSICAL... BODY LANGUAGE BRIEF

PURPOSE

To explain how to notice and read physical behaviours that reflect, reveal and imitate internal thinking.

OUTCOMES

On completion of this chapter the reader will be able to:

1   Describe the relevance of positioning
2   Explain how speed and positioning translate into other modes
3   Explain the effect of high and low energy states

METHOD

Providing ideas, examples for the reader to actively use by observation of people allowing the reader to develop means of analysing basic observable behaviour.

This includes:

1   Exercises in observation of positioning and relationships
2   Exercise rapport

Albert Mehribian (1968, 1972) suggested that information is carried in each mode of communication in clear proportions. He was helping us to understand that we derive meaning from a message from observable body language and voice quality.

Albert Mehribian

The Content (ie the words alone)	7%
Vocal Influences (i.e tones, accents, stresses, pauses, intonation, rhythm and pitch)	38%
Non-verbal Influences (i.e. posture, gestures, facial expressions, eye movements, muscle & skin colour change)	55%

Figure 14 Mehribian Communication Proportions

He was also aware that the social context of any interaction was relevant to meaning. I have gone further in suggesting this is a dynamic inter / intra personal and cultural process. That is, the inner perceptions and history of a person will act dynamically on their perceptions and these interact with the inner perceptions of others in a complex dance of social negotiation. As I quoted Stienbeck in Chapter 2 - "People do not want information, they want confirmation."

This chapter deals with those observable behaviours that are often not part of the intended message.

4.1 Position

How we position ourselves and react, the distance we stand from others and our eye contact are driven by internal process around expectations, beliefs, capabilities, physiology and energies. I will introduce the structure and development of basic preferences in some of these internal processes from the work of Eyzenck and Kelly, see outlined below the models and structures of how traits form from innate predispositions. (See also Chapter 6 - Typologies)

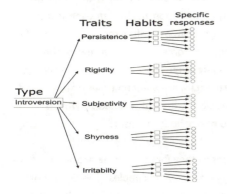

The developmental psychological research strongly suggests that in the early years babies will imitate and strive for basic need fulfilment. They are born with innate physical predispositions; preferences for where we are on scales like Extraversion-Introversion, Stable-Neurotic that Eyzenck calls Traits. We are also born with preset fears, desires and reactions. As these preferences react with our world they create further sets of preferred reaction styles which extend into specific behaviours which may become habits.

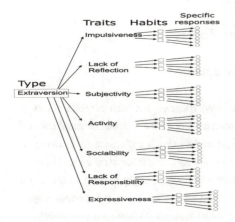

Figure 15 Eyzenck's Theory of Trait Development

This is extremely useful in survival terms; babies are born with a basic tool kit for survival and develop special skills to fit the environment into which it is born. If the environment changes from the one our parents faced, the baby is able to develop specialised skills to thrive in the new environment.

Children learn that their movements have an effect, though the link seems magical at first; they come to understand how an action is linked to an outcome. Soon, although they cannot see the direct relationship they begin to believe that their intentions, ideas, feelings and states have an effect on others and can produce actions from others. Most children develop the ability so well that they can imagine how others see them.

This sense of related actions without physical connection often generates a sense of the magical, which may go unchecked for validity and can stay with many into adult life. A football fan watching a match on television, might lean over as if to encourage a ball into the net. A bowler might lean over after they have let go of the ball to apparently encourage its trajectory. Someone might screw up their face if they are angry about something on television. These apparently nonsensical acts suggest that body language and internal state are sometimes intimately linked. It is hard for us to hide this process especially if we are distracted by what is happening in an event, becoming unaware of our body language.

So people often betray their internal states as they focus on some action or problem. The following illustration will give you some examples. The discomfort produced by being too close to someone can cause a person to forget how their face or body is changing.

Gross Positioning - Comfort Zones

First the gross positioning - the fairly obvious actions.

In the illustration on the following page I have mapped out each person's zones of comfort; the inner ring denotes the minimum distance a close personal friend may comfortably be from the person. The middle ring is a distance that colleagues, casual friends etc can be for comfort and the outer ring is for strangers. There is also a much bigger zone of comfort for enemies, which might extend to the town or even the limits of the country. Below is an example of how two people might have very different comfort zones and how an interaction between them might progress.

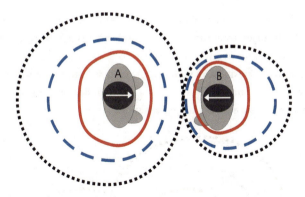

Figure 16 Comfort Zones Intimate, Friend, Stranger "Culture Stages 1"

Initially these two were at a comfortable distance from each other.

Person A was European, a man, 43 years old, not athletic and a professional. These parameters can change the shape and size of zones. It will tell us who, in a group, is used to whom, and sometimes that they are from different societal backgrounds.

Person B was from Dubai, athletic and gregarious. Within seconds the positioning progressed as shown below.

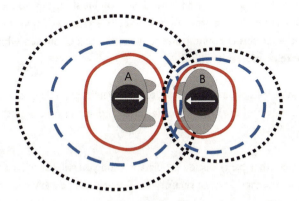

Figure 17 Comfort Zones – Invasion "Culture Stages 2"

A was uncomfortable, although he was diplomatic, he showed signs of stress and leant backwards, unfortunately giving the appearance that he was disdainful of his colleague B. Eventually he turned sideways on, increasing the 'focal distance', the distance at which his eyes were able to focus comfortably on B. B, now back at the edge of A's stranger zone remains there until A becomes more comfortable. A is tolerating B's intrusion into their 'Friend Zone' but not into their 'Intimate Zone' to prevent raising an issue with a stranger before they know more about them. It might be uncomfortable for A for a short while but it prevents an act of rejection before A is sure that is the right action.

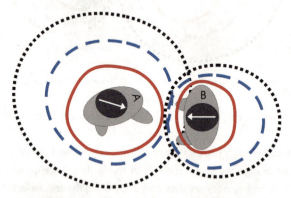

Figure 17a Comfort Zones - Artificial Coping "Culture Stages 3"

A now feels he has sent a message and is coping. B may feel that A is still rejecting him a little since A has also moved his head back on his shoulders to increase the focal distance further. Even a little training – see Exercise Eye Contact - could have prepared A for this encounter and reduced the risk of offence, while making A actually more comfortable with B.

The signal that tells us we are too close, too familiar to something is that the small fluid movements, e.g, of the neck, become stiffer and less in tune with the person's other actions.

Lesson – let the other party decide on distance and you will learn a lot about how they view you, their level of security/confidence and possibly even something about their culture.

Our interpretations sometimes say more about our own paradigms and beliefs than the realities.

Grouping - Spontaneous

Even more obvious is the pattern in which groups organise themselves. In the illustration below, pick out the relationship of person A to the rest of the group and see if you can tell who is welcome and who is not, who is protecting/responsible for whom etc.

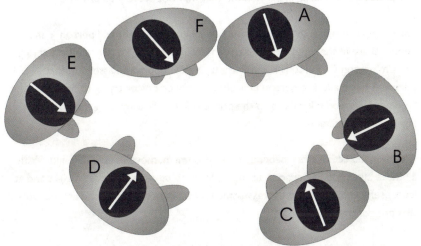

Figure 18 Grouping – Spontaneous

A Scanner would start to take in the possible relationships for future evidence and regard persons A, C and D as holding some form of power. Person A may have some intention towards B (notice the foot) and person B may be colluding with C as C takes a protective posture between A and B.

Person F seems to be submitting to A for the moment at least and D is comfortably watching for the outcome, safe at a distance. Person E is the odd one out, excluded by foot directions of F and D from the group. E is watching D for an entry and clearly this gives D an implication of power. However, if person E is deferring to D their proximity suggests that there is a separate reason for the interchange. The head position of E, being forward, suggests they want person D to engage with them instead of the group.

Clearly you may have a different and perfectly valid interpretation. However, if we are untrained and unprepared, **our interpretations sometimes say more about our own paradigms and beliefs than the realities.** So we need to be clear about our own prejudices and instincts when working as a Scanner. Our instincts will be useful; they will point the way to where we might try focussing. We then have to check them out with other evidence, even if it is subjective at first; to cross check we must see the action from a completely different vantage point. So try another explanation in a subjective style to illustrate, throw into contrast where our prejudices are filling in information that may not actually be present.

For example, imagine this group is outside a bar at midnight and person A and person B are in the middle of a disagreement. Person B is a police officer trying to calm person C. Persons E and F are trying to support an assertion that person A has made and person D is another police officer trying to listen to their argument. Person F is talking to the police officer while watching person C for any signs of escalation.

Clearly a subjective story depends on environment, movement and sound. With all these clues your assertions are more likely to be right or close to right and at least useful. Now put the two assessments together, deleting those assessments that are contradictory.

Immediately the Scanner can see that the high speed trouble spots are C and F. The officer D would be advised to distract F, using A as part of the conversation, move even closer to C and to maintain eye contact with both C and F to match their behavioural frequencies.

A's head is back and C is leaning forward slightly. F's position indicates he is hiding slightly behind A and this may suggest that F's internal pressure to attack is rising. Not shown here are any walls, escape routes or other groups that might influence the group.

All of this can be changed by observation of skin tone, breathing, size and height of the individuals, speed of speech etc. The most important information, **TIME**, is also missing - how they move, nerves, strategic position changing; this is where we notice, e.g, someone moving, perhaps awkwardly, to get themselves into a better position. **In business, tribal (perhaps even pack) instincts still seem to operate.**

However, this serves to give you an idea of signals that can be picked up even from positioning. This kind of training is pretty basic for police officers and in business it can show us how tribal, even pack, instincts operate. Although there are differences throughout the world there are also many similarities driven by our genome and the logic of being in tribes that create a human cultural set of behaviours. Some of the greatest differences were apparent in plains tribes where the individual is often left alone in dangerous situations with great responsibilities compared to someone immersed in family and teams sharing responsibilities in a physically safe environment.

The same processes of familiarisation seem to run in the same order when we meet. "What are you? Who are you? How similar are you to me and mine? How shall I interact with you? Any differences in this process seem to be mostly in the speed of each stage and the certainty required before moving on.

Imagine the group above now in a boardroom discussing a take-over and run your imagination through the possibilities. Here is the difference with Scanner – NONE of this is taken as fact, it is used as untested evidence to support other observations.

In a later section we will be looking at maturity; at when the behaviour was first encoded. For this exercise imagine the group are 12 year olds in a playground or 80+ and each imagining will add ideas. This is the level of mental work we run for every situation and it has to be run in seconds to allow time to keep up with the action as well. There are exercises that help us in this at the end of the book and it is not as hard as it seems.

Gross Information

When the client enters the room there is a mass of very helpful information. Look at these next pictures and draw out as much information as you can from each. Are they resistant, nervous, eager, here because they were sent etc?

Notice the lines of force, where the weight is going and how the chest is presented.

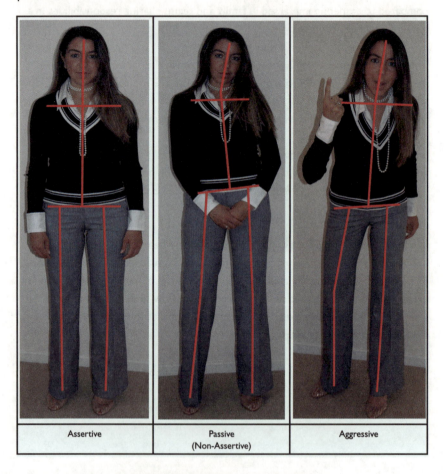

Assertive	Passive (Non-Assertive)	Aggressive

Figure 19 Gross Information - Assertive vs Non Assertive

Pushing your chin up will raise your eye level and this action is deep automatic behaviour, very primitive even primordial, it portrays a sense of status and influence. When we feel vulnerable we may automatically seek to lower our eye level in submission 'to avoid challenging others'. (Also see Typologies).

So how would you expect these people to behave?

You will need to know why he is standing there, why she is pointing, what just happened, the tone of voice they are using - the whole context. Notice that the man on the left is really erect; his backbone must be as straight as it will go. What about the woman on the right?

Figure 20 Standing Man

Figure 21 Pointing woman
Istockphotos Inc.

Body Language Display

In the boardroom there may be a very brief flick of a nod towards the person who is apparently in charge. This can be a shock when you see the gruff and apparently dominant CEO lower their head to someone else. Often it will be because they are more technical, have more recent information or are more politically connected. So watch out for which subject is dominated by whom on which topic.

Look at the aerial view of two cartoon characters on the next page. Imagine B is your client, who arrives and stands as shown:

Figure 22 I Don't Want to Tell You.

If this is the only evidence it might tell you, "There is something I don't want to tell you and I feel inadequate about it." What might it mean if B was the manager and A arrives for A's appraisal? What if A were a parent? If we can imagine all the other situations in which these body positions might occur, we start to get other possibilities. We also use this in maturity analysis; as we scan, we might find the closest fit to a similar situation is a parent 'telling off' their child. Though they are directors discussing a plan, it gives us insight into their current power positions and probable source of barriers and instinctual behaviour.

Imagine you have arranged to meet with someone and they arrive and sit like either person A or person B below.

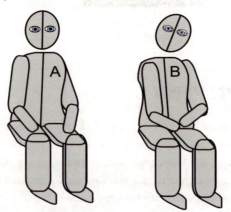

Figure 23 Assertive vs Non-Assertive

You might make some first pass assumptions about their attitude and personal strength. Notice the differences in their eyes. Taken simply, it seems straight forward; A seems confident and B unsure. A's body is upright, B is leaning forward with head bowed and hands in the lap. A's eyes are wide open and B's are slightly hooded.

Figure 24 Eyes 1

OK that was a simple example; now, a few minutes later?

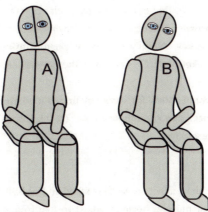

Figure 25 Assertive vs Non-Assertive Change

In the second set A has bent the head slightly back and the right pupil has contracted slightly.

Figure 26 Eyes 2

This would cause a Scanner to try to find out why there is a change; what is it about the situation or subject of discussion that has changed?

B, in the second set, has moved the hands out, moved the body forwards but kept the head in a subservient position while the left pupil has dilated and the eye hooding has subtly changed. We will deal with eye shape later but for now notice that the eye is half-way between a frown and a demur.

This posture is a warning signal for the Scanner and indicates we may be dealing with a Passive Aggressive, PA. PAs are primarily interested in getting their justice without being seen as assertive or responsible. For more information on PAs and many more personality styles see literature on 'Transactional Analysis', e.g, 'TA Today', Stewart & Joines. 'Games People Play', E Berne.

Posture

There is so much material on positioning that it would fill several books. However, we all have most of the information already coded into us by social exchanges from birth. To find out what a particular posture might mean, sculpt yourself into that posture. Be observant in copying, because even a small difference can be the key. When you have the posture, ask yourself, "How would I feel sitting/standing like this?" This may give the insight needed.

When you know what to look for, you may notice it when a Scanner shifts their posture during meetings to run this exercise. They are copying some aspect of someone else to gain insight.

Muscles

The way a person thinks affects how they stand and walk, if the way of thinking is frequent then their muscles begin to adjust to that frequent posture. In many cases we can tell a lot about a person simply from how their muscle structure shapes their posture, even when they are at rest.

Head Tilting

Even in open organisations with co-operative decision making, the ranking is often clear by how the heads are tilted. As a Scanner, if you want to disappear in a meeting without loss of position, make notes. Your head will be tilted down and eye access limited so there will be little attention on your rank until you are needed.

In the picture on the following page the head tilting is part of a 'to and fro' of mutual coercion. The man is trying to gain agreement from the woman and the woman is temporarily leaning backwards taking in what he is saying. Both heads are tilted in relation to the main body. The woman's lower body however is giving away that she is standing her ground and may not be pleased with the information she is receiving. The head in this position is fairly aggressive. Imagine you are trying to protect your head from a potential punch, like a boxer many people instinctively create this kind of angle so that the neck is better prepared for the imaginary punch.

Figure 27 Head Tilting - Istockphotos Inc.

Head tilting puts the head below the other person's head. An imaginary punch would have less effect and the throat, a vulnerable spot, is more protected. Demonstrating the fear of attack is a display of fear and is translated (generalised) into a display of respect, even subservience.

As you enter a room with others in it you can get a sense of what height you need to be and to whom your head should tilt. I have noticed that if someone dresses down, e.g, jeans or sports shirt, and enters a boardroom full of 'Armani' suits, with their head held high, there are two kinds of response.

1. *A slight turn of the shoulder that is intended to transmit a message. For example, and using an extreme to illustrate the point, "**You are an upstart, beyond your rank and you don't seem to know it**" The subtext is "..so this reaction is what you need to put you back in a place that I understand and then we will both be comfortable."*

2. **A focused look and a surge of interest seeming to say:
    "Interesting, you're confident without all the trappings".** The subtext
    is "You obviously either don't care about how you look or you have something so
    useful you can get away with dressing that way."

Obviously separating the group so quickly into dominating or interested is very
useful for us. However, I don't enjoy looking unkempt and there may not be
someone else to provide the provocation. So another method is to tilt the head
as you approach and then raise it as they start to talk, (if they bother talking
to you at all) you will get the same reaction style. They will first assess you as
submissive and then find you are quite happy to look them straight in the eye.
This can be quite disconcerting for some people so take care.

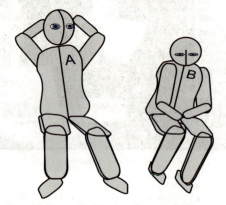

Figure 28 Sitting – Confidently vs Camouflaged Extremes

Camouflage is a vital aspect of scanning. It is important that as an observer we
can observe with a minimum of influence on others until we need it.
Looking at the example above, it is quite clear which person is trying to hide and
which is more confident.

What specific things can we notice? Try sitting in these positions. How do you
feel, what small detail can you notice?

A   Head erect, body tilted back, legs apart, staring eyes.
B   Head tilted down, knees together, feet underneath you, eyes averted.

Head tilting is a primal behaviour that is clear in many creatures, not just humans. Many animal behavioural text books will cover the subject.

SO WHAT?
People find it very difficult to hide head tilting, especially if they are suddenly distracted as a new person comes close to them or as the situation suddenly changes and they are unsure of how to react.

Arrogance
For the purpose of learning, a useful exercise to illustrate this point is the modelling of arrogance. It is vital to be clear that this does not mean being rude, it simply means being supremely confident that you are right. You do not need to prove anything or be apologetic. Typically you will find that short term you get preference, however, later it can result in a situation where it is very difficult to recreate a collaborative relationship, e.g, a teaching relationship with a student. See Example 7 below.

Example 7 Arrogance - Posturing

Some five years ago I arrived at a hotel to register, I joined a queue and those in front of me all got the same speech, "We are double booked and we have to send you to another hotel by taxi just a mile away." I needed to be in that hotel because I was lecturing in a conference centre next door at 9:15 the next day. Pulling myself up to my tallest, avoiding any eye contact so that no questions could be put to me, I arrogantly announced that I had heard the message and it was impossible for me so, "I want you to find a way to get me the room I have contracted with you." I then proceeded to check my mobile phone messages while the unfortunate receptionist tried to attract my attention. There were others waiting behind me.

Finally I finished my 'call retrieving' and was given my room key. "Thank you" I said as I still gave no eye contact and whisked off to my selfish bed. Not ethical? I agree and I made my apologies to the receptionist just 20 minutes later, explaining my 150 mile journey and tiredness. I was forgiven; thank you.

I explained my research in people systems and asked what they made of my behaviour. "I have some rooms and it is hard to choose who to give them to, you just seemed so sure of yourself, I didn't feel I could object, it was easier to go along with you. I didn't like it." Clearly arrogance can affect relationships badly and is not usually useful, however it can help to protect us from being automatically deferential if that is also unhelpful..

SO WHAT?

If we understand that a person's power has a lot to do with these simple tricks, we can overcome them and understand the internal group structure that probably surrounds them.

Arrogance done badly has a four-stage effect on others.

1. Initial   surprise and commonly conformance
2. Short term   resentment
3. Medium term deference and/or compliance
4. Long term   disrespect/anger

If the receptionist had been a Scanner he could have remained silent until I gave eye contact. If I did not, he could have dealt with the next person in line until I was ready to engage in a debate. Alternatively he could have done some other administration work while waiting for me, or simply given me the same "other hotel" speech without worrying about whether I heard it or not.

An experienced Scanner might have used personal space to cause me to feel off balance, see 'Proximity Zones' in the section on 'Position'. With that achieved they would then ask me a question I could not answer to dig under the apparent confidence and then deliver the "So what makes you special?" kind of speech. Moving quickly into perhaps a complimentary room upgrade at the other hotel to finish me off. He would probably add that they would send a taxi to pick me up in the morning as an assumptive close.

4.2 Speed

People seem to operate at different speeds. A popular questionnaire, Myers-Briggs, claims to measure some of the basic preferences of a person, which would suggest the relative speed and energy in their neurons. Carl Jung, a psychologist and psychotherapist in the same era as Freud, described scales of personality types, (see Storr 1983) some based on these phenomena. Understanding this can help us to understand their timing and something about a quality of their thinking, evaluations and the likelihood of them listening and building rapport. In addition, sudden changes in speed help us to know where their energy is used and what is important to them.

I have already explained that brains are built to react at relatively different speeds. If we are working with what If we are working with what Eysenck (see section 4.1) called a 'Stable' and we behave in an excited way, changing the subject frequently, there is a tendency for the stable to regard us as trivial.

Conversely, we might regard them as slow-witted or not interested in what we have to say. When one works in business or management for a while one tends to put these assumptions away and to realise that the style does not say much about either seriousness or interest.

Security of Reading
*The core message, again, is that **calibration is vital.** No one aspect of behaviour can explain what is happening; it is the changes, in relation to the context and content of what is happening that provides a secure interpretation.*

However, if someone is usually excited and becomes slow, with associated body language perhaps sitting back, then there is often some lack of external engagement at that point. I have noticed that when directors pretend to be disinterested, this is often the first act they put on. We need to look at the whole body action and notice any alignment/misalignment between action and subject under discussion.

Manipulation

Stuart, a CEO of a multi-national IT company, said he would let me into his secret and explained that you have to "...build people up, then knock them down twice, then build them up, then begin to do it randomly..." He said the first changes in reward were designed to let them know how bad and good it could get. Making it random made them insecure and you could then get more control. I had already met this idea from the work of B F Skinner on 'reinforcement schedules'. These are used in the timings of slot machines (one-armed bandits) to obvious great effect.

While the morality of this is, for me, unacceptable, short sighted and old fashioned, it cannot be denied that it works for a great deal of people in the short term and often that is all they want. For a Scanner it is vital that we notice this mechanism and compensate for it in ourselves and the reactions of others.

Back to Stuart, our faking CEO: the Scanner will notice that the person has moved body position, usually to a casual position, and changed their whole demeanour in an attempt to persuade the other side they are genuinely cool towards the discussion. However, a foot or a blush or a change in speed will give it away.

One Scanner may pick out something another misses; sometimes the speed change is very abrupt. Clues are that the demeanour is too perfect or held artificially in position just a little too long. It produces what we call the 'mannequin effect'. If you are concentrating, the person looks artificial, frozen in a posture like a mannequin posed in a shop window.

CONTROLLING THE FOCUS

Provocative Interrupts - The Columbo

If they are being unresponsive the Scanner will intentionally make a crass or annoying interrupt, "More tea?", when there isn't any and no-one is drinking tea. They may start pulling out irrelevant papers, interrupting then having nothing to say. The purpose is to watch the person to notice if they artificially maintain their posture, which looks really incongruous (out of place) and is a real 'give-away', or break into another posture. The change will also show the internal state of mind of the client.

Often the artificial posturing will then be clearer, the person appears created, as if they were a mannequin being controlled remotely or by someone inside. I believe this is a useful way to view them, they are being controlled by a series of sub identities, each jostling for prominence and to be heard. You may notice them moving from one inauthentic pose to another in a series of moral cameos, e.g, "I am incredulous", "I am outraged", "I must be true to my staff". They move into the 'Cliché Robot' effect. If the client is becoming hard to read – it may be that they are behaving so inauthentically that the sequence of postures has no apparent rational connection; we can't make sense of what they really feel or think. They may move from one extreme emotion to another and it appears very artificial. Provocative interrupts can distract them long enough to work out their actual intent(s).

A word of warning here, **it is best to prepare your client for these provocative interrupts,** otherwise they may make their own response in a nervous way and cause the other side to have an escape. Simply explain before the meeting that you may do this.

I have worked with some clients who know the process well and still find it impossible to keep quiet at that moment. In this instance I have used their interrupt to create more trivial conversation and while they are wondering what is happening watched the other side's reaction to them. This can also be used to bring both sides together in a fairly superficial way; as you become the common enemy they get on better with each other. 'The enemy of my enemy is my friend'. I think this was Sun Tzu, 'The Art of War'. Although it may seem superficial, it can often be enough to begin a more productive dialogue.

We have called this technique the 'Columbo' after the apparently bumbling antics of Lieutenant Columbo from the TV series, who appeared to be absent minded and unintelligent so that he could get the criminal relaxed enough to make a mistake. "Crazy like a Fox."

4.4 Timing/Energy

A "When telling a joke, what is the most important... "
B "Timing"
A "...thing?"   Unknown author

Timing can be valuable if you want to be sure your audience has taken in what you want them to take in or for some of the audience to hear and not others. It is equally important to control listening if you want everyone present to hear and understand at the same time. I often do demonstrations of this in training, see Example 8.

Example 8 Timing

I was asked to work with a group who felt they were not as effective as they could be. I interviewed the Chairman before the meeting and gained his acceptance that I could interrupt whenever appropriate.

The meeting consisted of a group of 20 managers and the chair. I first calibrated several speakers' timing and speed of thought.

It quickly became clear that the chairperson always seemed to work out what he was going to say, said it without allowing any interruption and expected a few seconds of silence when he finished. If he did not get the silence he would start again, even interrupting the new speaker. He soon got everyone trained to weigh his words carefully and they all held a few seconds of respectful silence when he stopped speaking. A clever ploy, as Inspector Clouseau of the Sûreté would say.

Following the silence he expected everyone to talk among themselves and then he would take over again before anyone could try to gain control of the meeting or get the attention of the group.

A series of people had tried to interrupt him and had asked for my intervention several times. However, the Chairman moved the meeting on before they could complete their request and certainly before I could respond.

So I watched and waited for the inevitable microsecond when his attention would waiver and the group were supposed to begin to mumble to each other. Everyone has this blind spot; it seems to be a moment of gathering the material for the next idea. One manager I met ended tirades with a series of clichés so that it covered up his blank moment – very clever.

This Chairman, though, showed his blank spot by dropping his focus on the group for microsecond, see Fig 29 speech timing.

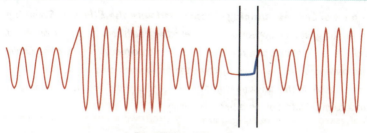

Figure 29 Speech Timing
A visual representation of the Chairman's speech pattern, showing the interruptible moment (in blue) just after his pause.

At that moment I knew he would be focussed internally and I announced "I will speak up whenever the Chairman takes a breath." The room erupted in laughter; everyone knew instantly that there was a way to interrupt after all. However, the Chairman was confused, he had not heard a word I said and wanted to know what everyone was laughing at.

He came to me later and asked what happened and I went through it as I have here. Luckily he laughed and we have worked together regularly since. This Chairman was an expert in timing, felt complimented to hear how effective he had been and wanted new ways to achieve a hearing without discouraging or alienating the audience.

SO WHAT?

Listening and working out the timing of everyone in a group will enable you to ensure everyone has heard important points, to get attention when you need it, to ensure your client has been heard properly and to gauge the energy and commitment of a group.

To do this we need to be quiet, watch and listen to everyone, without being distracted by the content. We need to mentally create an annotated map of everyone's timing. A will be periodic, B will always talk after C, D will interrupt for effect at the key moments, E will only speak when addressed directly and so on.

To achieve this you will need to clear your mind, see exercise 'The Brick' for meditation and 'Eyes' for taking in a lot at once.

Ethics

A key part of Scanner training is concerned with the Ethics of Scanning and reporting. It may appear that we are acting unethically in causing an interrupt, especially the style of interrupt above. However, I had already calibrated the Chairman and was convinced that he would welcome the provocation as a way forward. It is clear that some people in this situation would be offended and the Scanner may need to fail their task to avoid intrusion on a person's dignity.

The example also illustrates that people have a space for listening and a space when they do not. We need to know about those spaces to ensure messages are heard and understood.

4.3 Context

James Herbart (1824) also in Adams (2007) talked about stages of learning (read 6.3 Architypes / listening in this context) and broke it down into several stages that we have condensed into: preparation to learn, the learning and recapping. This generated the phrase, "Tell them what you're going to tell them, tell them, then tell them what you told them", for trainers and presenters.

The idea is that we need to prepare the person by having them prepare a place in their memory for information before we give them the information. We then deliver the information according to their expectation and, after receiving it, they then need to take time to close down the input and file the material away; so we tell them the character of what we have said so they can check it is what they expected and file it away with confidence.

To gain access, and have someone remember, we need first to give context so that they know where to put the information in their mental organisation. There is more about this later in '5.1 Language/Because/So'.

Illustrated in the diagram below are the levels an idea has to pass through to go from our concept to another person's memory. Internally it is affected by our physical state, then coloured by our experience and prejudice: it is only as complete a communication as our knowledge can make it. If we don't really understand the principles of quantum mechanics it would be hard to explain something about it. Finally, we may not give the communication enough importance or energy because we have other priorities or we may slant the message to get across some sub message, e.g,"I love you","I disapprove of you", etc.

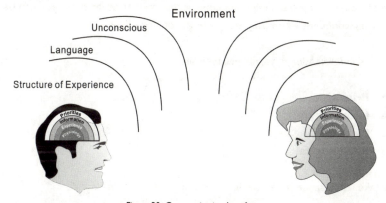

Figure 30 Communication Interference

Once it leaves our mind it then enters the joint social context of our shared experience, language barriers, unconscious behaviours, then it enters the environment, which may be noisy or distracting.

Then it starts its journey back down through the same barriers for the other person. It is not surprising that so many communications fail. Imagine all this in a highly threatening situation, energies are high and alternatives to our message present themselves in a confusion of scary threats. People often choose the most frightening alternative interpretation, because when we are not sure which of many things will happen we choose the worst. The logic is, if you imagine the worst you are prepared for and are not caught out by, that most frightening scenario.

Imagine you are frail and sitting in your house alone late at night. You hear a creak, a door in the hall is slowly opening, it could be the cat or dog or a burglar with a knife. Which belief will make you safer, the burglar or the pet? If it is the pet, you're safe but if it is the burglar you have only seconds to defend yourself. On average our worst imagining will save us more often.

Hence, people break up because the other person probably doesn't love them, deals break down because the other side probably will not honour their promises or they might find ways to let you down. When is it being careful and when is it paranoia?

Be aware of the levels of communication breakdowns so that you can calibrate where the issue lies for each person. Remember they may feign a lack of understanding but by watching them cope at that level at other times you can be reasonably confident when they are 'putting it on' for effect.

Is the misunderstanding typically or atypically:

a **Priorities**
b **Information**
c **Experience**
d **Physiological**

I will take some space/time now to go through these in more detail.

a Priorities

You will get a sense of how important the subject is for each individual and this is about her/his real and politically motivated interest (they know they ought to be interested but they are not, so they pretend to be).

It is nearly impossible to give proper attention if your personal priorities outweigh work priorities. Imagine a parent worried about their child or a spouse worried about their partner, they are not going to be fully present, their mind may be partly elsewhere. Someone who is at risk may be more interested in how they appear than facts.

b Information

Do they actually know what is happening? We can directly test this but by watching body language it is fairly easy to get the clues.

c Experience

Do they seem to cope easily with shifts of level of discussion? Are they comfortable with sudden changes. This will indicate their level: of intelligence, flexibility and probably breadth of experience in dealing with different situations.

d Physiological

They may be tired, worried or late. These things will be signalled in their energy states. Again a low energy state may be normal for someone; we are looking for indications that it may not be normal for them. They will be making small mistakes, dropping things or slurring words when they are not concentrating. They may seem distracted or impatient or confused unduly. A person will cope with life at whatever level they normally operate. So if their coping is failing it may indicate tiredness or confusion.

4.5 Environment

The environment can contribute to misunderstanding and to comfort or lack of comfort. In noisy environments some of the more subtle messages we observe may be obscured. If you decide you need to hear a particular person more clearly, say so and shift your position. You will know from the overview, Chapter 2, from whom you need these subtle signals.

It is important that you should not sit in the corner, it can reflect and distort sounds. Ensure you can move about, don't get trapped between two dominating characters. Don't drink alcohol, obviously. Finally, if you can't get enough data because the environment is noisy or you can't see people properly, signal to your client as soon as possible that you are unable to do your work in those conditions.

As with many things, unhelpful environments can sometimes be turned to advantage. A noisy environment tends to cause those who are most eager to lean forward and to become more insecure about the process.

I understand from a colleague that some industries are renowned for setting up unexpected and difficult environments and I reproduce here a story he relayed to me so that you can be aware of such manipulations and not be thrown by them.

Standing your ground, avoiding manipulation

Manipulation is often about using something the person wants, desires, fears, their goals, dreams etc, to get them to behave in a way that the manipulator would prefer.

When you start to get changes in groups there may be a time when some aspect of the group, fear, discomfort etc causes someone to try to manipulate you. You may find you have to choose between losing the client and losing your space to move and operate.

Clearly scanning takes time to really appreciate and your client may not always understand why you need space or access. If you lose the right to be the expert, and your scope is constrained too much, you will fail. Of course you will lose the business and access anyway so the choice is normally quite clear – stay professional, if the only choice is to lose the business, it is better to leave ethically and with clarity.

Negotiation/Manipulation

Standing your ground can be difficult and it is important to know when it is appropriate. I have reproduced a true story on the following page to illustrate how one leader stuck to his requirements and maintained the dignity of his team and his client – it may not always work this way; each person has their own unique style.

It is a useful exercise, if you have time, to read the next example and work out what are the key components of what he did that we need in these situations and what were unnecessary, even unhelpful.

Example 9 Negotiate? Part I

I cite this to advise Scanners to be aware that when they are working for a client, there is no off time until they are out of touch all together. The work requires concentration and energy. The mark of a good Scanner is that they go to bed early the night before. The test of an experienced Scanner is when they have been unable to go to bed early and they still turn in a great service. As Sun Tzu, 'The Art of War', advises us, "If you must engage in battle after a long march, make sure it is the enemy who has marched." (Not your own people)

A large corporate (company A) arranged for the supplier (company B) to visit them in their country and agreed to handle all their accommodation and transport. Company B arrived at the airport and were picked up. They expected to go to their hotel and have time to chat, shower and prepare for a meeting the next day.

The car arrived instead at company A's head office and company B were invited for an informal meeting with the executives of company A.

They had a warm reception and after a few drinks and some pleasant exchanges relations seemed to be proceeding well. The chairman of A arrived, clearly a man of great gravitas and he invited everyone into the boardroom. As soon as everyone was seated negotiations began.

The B people were unprepared and began to explain but the chairman said, "I am sure we can, with goodwill, get this all done now. I have been called to urgent talks with my staff in another city and it would assist me greatly. Otherwise I do not know when I will be able to complete these talks. Gentlemen?"

SO WHAT?

However prepared one is, there is always a chance of being caught off guard. Prepare your 'check-ins' see 'Language'. If you haven't seen John Cleese in 'Fawlty Towers', it contains exaggerations of well observed behaviour. In the situation described above Mr Cleese might, as he did in 'Gourmet Night' simply have fainted away on the spot to avoid the issue. Clearly we can't faint when we don't know what else to do, but we can have a need to go to the toilet, giving us time to think about how to handle the situation or to have a call come in on a mobile (even if it is switched off, silent alarm).

Perhaps a more business-like solution would be to use an ethic already stated by the other side as one in which they believe and are invested and turn it around as in Example 9 part 2.

Example 9 (continued) Negotiate? Part 2

B "Of course your time is of great concern to us and I am sure ours is to you. I would like to start by thanking you and your staff for our welcome. You would not want or expect our staff to present less than effectively. We must have a few minutes to reduce tomorrow's presentation for you so that we can complete efficiently this evening. Do you have a hospitality area or place for us to work?"

If this is a prospective client and the business is vital company A may now force the issue with:

A "We are aware of the short notice for both sides so we will bear with any lack of fluidity in your presentation."

B "I thank you for that, perhaps we could start then with a list of your expectations from this shortened meeting."

A "You know our expectations."

B "Thank you, if they remain unchanged from our briefing last week, I believe I do. Your excellent hospitality has caused the need for a brief comfort break, which I must take now. As the lead here, I don't want my colleagues to continue without me. Please (signalling to his team) leave this room now and wait for me in reception. I also need to take an update from HO before we begin. Excuse me gentlemen, we will be back in 10 minutes."

It is a high-risk strategy that falls just short of the greater risk of entering into negotiation unprepared.

It is vital that you know how strong you are today, what expectations the client has and how you can match or, if necessary, modify their expectations.

Is what you are doing, standing your ground on ethics or being selfish about your needs? List the things you need and update the list when you discover new needs so that eventually you have a clear list of needs upon which you can agree, even contract, with your client before you start. It will be unique for you but here is a starter list:

Sample List of 10 Scanner Needs

1 To be free from any requirement to be involved in the content of the meeting.

2 To be able to arrive in time, peacefully.

3 To know your client's required outcomes and to understand what your client believes are the other side's desired outcomes.

4 To ask questions (however stupid they appear) and not have your client's team interrupt before they are answered.

5 If you are introduced, to be introduced as a facilitator or friend or spare note taker. Never as a psychologist or negotiator. Sometimes the other side may know of you and have formed their own opinion; then it can't be avoided. If you have completed formal Scanner training you may introduce yourself as a Scanner defined as: A professional group facilitator.

6 To give reports in confidence and in private. Avoid the situation where the client announces your role and asks you to tell everyone who and what you are. It may boost your ego but it often alienates someone in the group and demeans the process.

7 To be allowed to be in a place where you can observe effectively.

8 To be given the right to halt proceedings. You may not always get this but if you need to tell your client something before things go too far then you may need this courtesy.

9 To be allowed to brief your client about Provocative Interrupts before any meeting.

10 To know as far as possible who and how many people will be attending.

I have used the term 'other side' often to denote a faction who is not the primary client, often the faction may be a subset of your client's; their staff, co-directors etc. The other side may even be their spouse although this is more the remit of the family counsellor.

4.6 Eyes
Eye Accessing

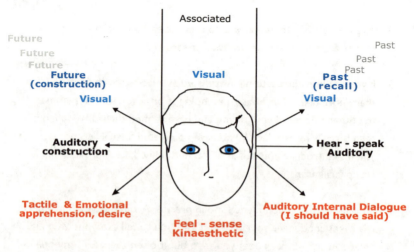

Figure 31 Eye Accessing

In the discipline of NLP - Neuro Linguistic Programming (Bandler and Grinder) - much is made of the way we seem to represent the world internally on a point for point basis. This is illustrated by the way our eyes move when we think of something. They seem to actually move as if they are examining a model of what they are thinking about.

In a therapy known as EMDR the practitioner tries to connect a potentially irrational memory with other memories/beliefs by asking the patient to think of the original memory. When they have some link with the memory the practitioner helps them to move their eyes left and right quite quickly but at a comfortable rate. The results are that the patient's thoughts roam 'bilaterally' from left to right and back, accessing pathways in their brain that are linked even slightly with the original thought.

This causes the patient to process and sort out their memories in much the same was as they are doing in REM (Rapid Eye Movements) sleep. REM is that part of sleep when the sleeper's eyes move rapidly as if they are following the action of some dream. It would seem, then, that there is some direct and powerful link between where in our brains we are thinking and our eye position or perhaps the eye movement stimulates the nerve cells, or vice versa, in some way that relates to the way the memory is organised.

With many people it is possible to calibrate (notice) where they look when they are thinking about the past, the present and the future. It is quite common that if they are thinking about images they look up, for words they look sideways or straight on and for other senses/feelings they look down. In my experience the visual accessing is fairly accurate, however if someone is remembering an emotional conversation they may flick between directions as they sense either the words, feelings or an image of the event. There also seems to be fairly regular past, present and future places although my experience is that occasionally this is different for each individual and yet consistent for them: if they look up to the right for imagining a scene in the future they will always look there for that, etc.

This is one of the most persuasive and easy to demonstrate pieces of NLP/ Scanner evidence. To demonstrate to a client we first calibrate them, tell them where they are looking for e.g, the past and then ask them to recall something in detail without looking in that direction. Some people can do this by attempting to disassociate their eye movements from their imagining but they find it difficult and this difficulty alone demonstrates the reliability of the effect. For a good introduction, well illustrated grounding in NLP, I recommend Sue Knight's book 'NLP at Work' or any of the John Seymour calibration series.

SO WHAT?

It must be obvious that if someone looks at a certain spot when talking about say, their family, and later expresses they have concerns while looking at the same spot, there may be family issues involved. This is not, as my son would say, "rocket science".

By taking note of where people are looking when talking, we can get tremendous insights into when people are: concerned, trying to deceive, convinced, referring to someone specifically for permission etc. Clearly this is a great asset for a Scanner.

However hard the person tries to keep their body still they will flick an eye when there is a change over of ideas or a memory occurs to them. The term 'shifty-eyed' comes from people who avert their eyes or whose eyes dart around so much that it becomes difficult for us to notice relevant changes.

Basic Eye Character

> The movements of expression give vividness and energy to our spoken words. They reveal the thoughts and intentions of others more truly than do words which may be falsified.
>
> Charles Darwin

Exercise

People tend to pick up a lot from other's eyes; they have been called "the window to the soul". Take a look at the following two pictures, which one is friendly and welcoming. Which is a posed smile? How do you know?

Sometimes we know instantly, sometimes the difference is very subtle. It may seem as if there are as many eye shapes as there are people. However, there are some basic shapes that are very helpful for us.

Istockphoto 3924891   Figure 32 Poster Smile

EYES

Figure 33 Emotion in the Eyes

Most people can make their eyes appear hooded or wide and some people have a preference. This will only tend to give away their energy levels and internal states as they change from their preference. In addition someone with normally hooded eyes may be slow to react even though they might be bright and have lots of ideas. The converse might be true that someone with a wide-eyed, even wild look may have loads of attention energy but have little going on behind. So don't assume that eye state indicates attention. It may indicate their reaction speeds if they have one style most of the time.

Many people have prejudices about how a person appears, including their eye postures so we need to train ourselves to work on the evidence and this comes from triangulated observation as I explained in Chapter 1. What other things also occur as the client's eyes change from their norm to become lazier or more intense?

Have a look at Exercise Faces.

Changing from hooded to excited obviously denote energy changes. Someone pretending disinterest but whose open eyes became fully open like those on the right would be giving away their attention level.

It is fairly easy to make one's eyes appear one way or the other, for a short while, however, the person will leak out interest or disinterest in other ways; foot/finger tapping, slow or uninspired language use etc.

Eyes are the fastest most detailed access to emotional state. Watching a person's eyes will show microsecond reactions to what you are saying or the activity around them.

Right and Left Person

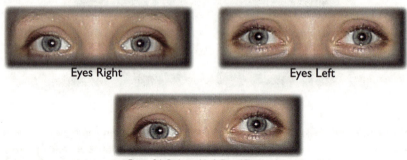

Eyes Right   Eyes Left

Figure 34 Right and Left Eyes (Chimeric)

Calibration is vital, the top two sets of eyes in Figure 34 'Right and Left eyes' are both from the same picture of a person. I have pasted two copies of their right eye together and two copies of their left (their eyes in normal context are shown underneath). The eyes left seem happier than eyes right yet this was the same person at the same time. There may be some connection between brain hemispheres and eyes but it is complex, see right/left brain a couple of pages on from this.

If someone predominantly hooded their eyes like the eye on the left in those in the figure 33 'Emotion in the Eyes' one might take them as a 'Stable'; a person who reacts slowly. If they were like those on the right more often the person would be excitable. However, these are again for the same person but at different times.

Other Right Left

Figure 35 Original Photograph

Figure 36 Right and Left Faces

In these pictures we have taken a single face – Figure 35 'Original Photograph' and, like the eyes on the previous page, cut and pasted both right sides together and both left in Figure 36 'Right and Left Faces'. It is obviously the same person but what is her mood?

Since it was taken from the same photo (this is called a Chimeric) she was in the same mood, yet we have shown these to several people and many have said that one seems more genuinely pleased to see you and the other younger and more aloof?

Perhaps you see other differences and my interpretation says more about me and my research subject than what she is thinking and feeling. Yet these reactions are real for the person reacting and have profound effects on how people are perceived.

Notice that the Right-Right face (shown on the left) looks more like the original. If you struggle to see any difference, look into the eyes for a while and imagine having a polite disagreement or try to guess the age of both independently. If you still struggle, don't worry, it can take time to become aware of the signals; that is what the training is about and this person has a fairly symmetric face chosen to make the point about subtle differences.

Right Left Brain

There is empirical and experimental (Sacks 1985) evidence of right/left differences. There is a vast, fast highway of communication between the right and left brain called the 'corpus callosum' (large body). The right and left can operate independently but a person's actions would appear confused if they did. We appear coherent and free from sustained significant internal messaging conflict because this formation enables high volume, high speed communication between the two halves.

When surgeons have cut the corpus callosum (used in the past to alleviate serious forms of epilepsy), preventing both sides of the brain from direct communication with each other, the result has been two distinct personalities both sharing, even fighting for control, in the same person.

I suspect we will find that the right specialises in parallel/holistic thinking and the left in translations, concrete serial/detail thinking.

A person's face is sometimes very different on the right from the left, although much of this may be due to genetics.

Here is the warning again; calibration, establishing the links between observation and action, is the only sure way of understanding relevance. Simple observation on its own can be misleading.
I believe it is possible to see different sides of a person's character by first focusing on one side of their face and then the other. Why this should be, I don't know, and in some people it can be quite extreme.

Try, in a conversation, to first talk to the right side, then the left, to see which gives you better rapport. This one exercise has revealed so much over the years about conflict and about who is the real person inside. I suspect one side is used as a mask or interface to the world and the other is more often the face of emotion. This is a really valuable way to know people.

If it has a link with brain specialisms, remember, to an extent the right brain controls the left side of us and vice versa, so the 'perceiving' side is going to be their left We see it on the right as we face them. Their 'judging' side will be on the left as we look at them.

We talk about people being predominantly 'ISH' or 'IS' (see Meta programmes in Chapter 6 Typologies); Perceiving or Judgemental (see also the work of Myers-Briggs, Eyzenck and Carl Jung).

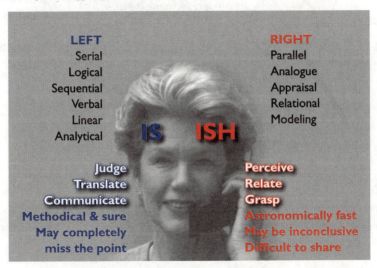

Figure 37 Right/Left Conceptual Specialisms

These terms are illustrative only, the reality is that the corpus callosum is a massive set of neurons which means both sides communicate so quickly it is difficult to be sure which side is responsible for what without a specialist scanning machine. In addition the signals from the eyes cross over under the brain.

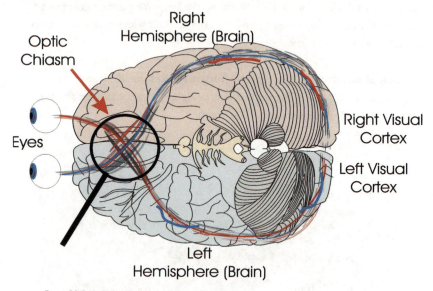

Figure 38 'Right Left – The Optic Chiasm'. The magnifying glass indicates Chiasm - not to scale.

Information from the right eye goes to the left visual cortex and vice versa. As they cross in what is known as the 'Optic Chiasm' some information is exchanged before that information goes back to register in the optic cortex.

I am unaware of any direct experimental evidence to suggest that eyes respond in sympathy with a person's right/left preference. However, the experience of working with hundreds of people suggests that there may be some feedback system at play, displaying their preferences. If this is eventually proven, then it will offer us a very fast way to understand the source of a person's feelings. If we calibrate their sense of being at ease or agitated, as we test their reactions to our looking at their right or left eye we can start to predict their reactions AND the source of those reactions.

I know that you believe you understand
what you think I said, but I'm not sure you
realise that what you heard is not what
I meant.

ROBERT McCLOSKEY

SOCIAL BEHAVIOUR
(LANGUAGE)

Chapter 5

SOCIAL BEHAVIOUR
(The use of language and creation of Coherent Self)

These Topics are concerned with :
Organising coping and power systems

PURPOSE
To explain the effect and use of language in a range of group interactions.

OUTCOMES
On completion of this chapter the reader will be able to:

1   Describe the benefit of recognising language structures
2   Explain how speed and intonation can denote personal preferences and positions
3   Explain how context can add or detract from clarity

METHOD
Provide ideas and examples for the reader to actively use in observation of people. This will allow the reader to develop means of analysing observable behaviour.

Note:
For the purpose of this book language is treated as a special form of behaviour, however the author recognises that language is many other things; a philosophy, a logical system and a science in its own right.

5.1 Language

The way we use language can radically change the outcomes we get. Recognising how others use it also tells us how they sort out the world. It indicates hundreds of ways people: differentiate, prepare themselves for discussions and confrontations, analyse what we say and decide on action.

Expertise in the use of language is a core essential for scanning. A great part of the training for the advanced Scanner is around logic, reason and rhetoric for good reason – language is our primary tool in reconciliation, persuasion and eliciting evidence.

> # Our emotions are based on our internal conversations.
>
> Based on Gross (2006)

Gross suggests that our emotions are based on our internal conversations which are constructed from the language of our culture. Jung believed that culture is a group neurosis. I believe that we can learn a lot about a person from the rhetoric they use; how it is constructed, the models they use and the hierarchy of importance placed on those models. E.g. Are individual needs primary or do the needs of the many outweigh the needs of the few?

Gross seems clear that our pride is involved with our anger. The process of anger rising is about a threat to our pride and must access an internal imagined or remembered dialogue. Talking with several clients it is clear that imagining how a conversation might have been different causes mental energy often to the detriment of the person's sense of well being. Whereas, **imagining how one might deal with a similar conversation in the future seems to cause less stress.** Language is used both to communicate and to think; the external reflects the internal but they are not always the same.

Positive Language

In writing about positive language power I am aware that G R Walther (1992) has created a definitive work on the subject. For a full understanding I refer the reader to it. As a brief introduction here are four examples.

Language Use for Scanners in Business

	A	B	C	D
	Linking Ideas	Absolute	Positioning Relevance	Context
Reduces % desired outcomes	**BUT**	**ALWAYS / NEVER**	**JUST**	**BECAUSE**
Increases % desired outcomes	**AND**	**OFTEN / SELDOM**	**REALLY**	**SO**

Table 2 Power Talk

It is helpful to know when our language will elicit information and when it might cause a shift in direction. So let's look at the four examples in more detail:

A   Linking ideas: But Vs And

"I am pleased with your progress but I need to talk with you today."

This But structure negates the compliment and implies there is a problem. Changing the word "but" to "and" makes the request to talk seem positive.

B   Absolute: Always Vs Often

"I always seem to have a problem completing tasks with you."

If you said this then clearly you would have an issue with this person and you would seem to believe there is no solution. Here we can try "often" instead and your statement then seems to allow for the possibility of a solution. Follow it by saying – "Perhaps I can change what I do to, in some way, suit you better?" and you are further from unhelpful and nearer to solution seeking.

C   Positioning relevance: Just Vs Really

"I just want to talk with you."

You may be trying to indicate that your request is not intended to be time consuming or difficult. It also carries the message that any outcome may be of small value; you are diminishing the contribution of the other person before they speak. Imagine replacing the word "just" with "really" as in:

"I really want to talk with you."
     This might sound harsh or forbidding. Instead try:

"I really need your advice."

D   Context: Because Vs So

This last example is more involved, perhaps more subtle. As I explained in a previous section, by giving people a context first, we prepare their minds for the information. If we give them the information before the "Why do I need to know this?" or "What will you want me to do with this?" they may not be able to balance the relevancies of the various bits of information as you say them and will be trying to guess what it is about.

This takes a lot of mental energy and they may not be listening to you very well and may even be forming a fear, based on a mistake, that causes them to put up resistance to you unnecessarily.

In this kind of example, it can go on for many pages before you find out the purpose. In murder mystery books, it might add to the suspense. In business it can be disastrous. Whether you use **"because"** or **"so"** is not of itself important, it is important that we recognise that "because" and "so" tend to indicate if you have put the context last or first.

"I need you to stop what you are doing and come with me to see the Director because we want to ask your opinion."

"The director and I would like your opinion, so could you stop what you are doing and come and help us now?"

For a fuller description of positive language see G R Walther.

Getting Action

When working in complex situations or with several people at once, it is important that we know what would help to create clarity of intent between all relevant parties. If we understand the context, the drivers, then we can apply a particular stimulus to move that context on to a desirable outcome. We have a lever to move on with our specific issues, which we often need to do our job. I have listed in Table 3 (context actions) some recommended actions from management training for each situation.

Signal / Content	Action	To lead you will need
Confusion / Chaos	Get priorities	Vision
New ideas	Provide support / training	Alignment / consultation
"Let's try that"	Get short term objectives	Energies / resources
Lack of cohesion	Hold planning sessions	Values / messaging / vision
Experimenting	Encourage / set standards	Boundaries / budgets

Table 3 Getting Action in Context

Messaging

If we discuss at the level of content without context there is a lot of opportunity for misunderstanding. To illustrate this have a look at Example 10 - Hidden Stories. This is an example of how a communication can go wrong when the context and/or belief systems have not been checked out and matched. Notice how understanding drifts further away despite the attempt of both parties to progress.

Example 10 Hidden Stories – Context Mismatch

Person A says (and thinks)	A hears...	B hears...	Person B says (and thinks)
We need to talk about promotions. **(Whom should we promote?)**	➡️	How should we decide who should be promoted?	⬇️
⬇️	We need a different kind of person promoted so they will bring about a new system.	⬅️	Yes I think we need a new system. (for deciding who should be promoted.)
I don't think so; the team we have got is ok. **(The sort of people we have are doing well?)**	➡️	The system we have used so far has worked.	⬇️
⬇️	We have upset those who have not been promoted.	⬅️	Our decisions have caused some bad feeling in the past. People do not understand our criteria for promotion.
Well it's hard, but we can't promote everyone. **Those who have not been promoted may feel hard done by.**	➡️	We're in charge and we don't have to explain our reasons.	⬇️
	I don't like you and I do not want to work with you.	⬅️	I think that is very high handed of you. You should not be so dictatorial.
Perhaps we had better discuss this another time. **I don't understand why you are so upset, let's have a break and try again later.**	➡️	I veto your involvement and have no more time for you.	Call me when you're ready to talk. I reject you too.

Table 4 Discussion Levels (Context Mismatch)

It seems pretty clear that there is a great deal of misunderstanding in the above conversation because each person has made assumptions.

The first assumption is about the context in which they are speaking:

Types of people **VERSUS** System of measurement

At this stage it would be much easier if they could stop and establish the context. If A asked, "What is it about the system you feel needs thought?" B would have a chance to explain their view and then be ready to hear that A also wants to talk about the criteria for promotion as well.

See Example 12 'Match, Pace, Lead' in Chapter 6 - Typologies for a version that is a more productive exchange.

F Leaders Who is leading what?

As explained before, we know who the leader is even if they are hiding in a group, by the glances of others towards them, even though it is sometimes very subtly done. We can also know them from their language and phrasing.

> A **leader** might say:
> "So Frank, you think we should go with this proposition."
> A **referent** (someone referring to a leader) might say:
> "So Frank, you think we should go with this proposition?"

The question mark indicates a down turn in emphasis on the front of the remark and an increase in the permission request quality. Birdwhistell (1970) has several coding systems to illustrate these changes. I will use my own system here to highlight the differences.

In the Example overleaf I have run words together to illustrate scripting, this is when a sequence of words all relate to a single cognitive or emotional concept. I use full stops to show slight pauses and capitals to show phrasing emphasis.

In everyday work we say we are checking the emotional commitment. More accurately it could be called checking "Soma commitment"; Soma as in emotive. I mean checking the emotional state of personal commitment along with, at the same time as, understanding the ramifications of that commitment.

Example 11 Leader Language

Leader – Knowing them from the style used

Leader:
"So...Frank, (attention first)...YOU think (check commitment (soma))... weshouldgowiththisproposition."(implied) - in accusative tone.

Referrent:
"SoFrank, (permission request)... youTHINK (opinion taking) we should? gowiththisproposition?"(intense eye contact) Notice that the leader's script was the whole of "we should go with this proposition".

It illustrates here that s/he is used to using phrases that are about interest around group commitments. When the referrent runs together the words "you think", emphasising THINK s/he primarily wants to know what is the decision and the "go with this proposition" phrase is clearly separated, almost an afterthought.

Leaders communicate the direction and speed of energy required, the vector of the organisation. As such they create the issues for management to manage.

Cliff Edwards, speech to "Creative Leaders In Industry" 1989

On Message
When a people leader says "Let's go" s/he also indicates where, when, how, why, who and what. This is not always done with language. S/He will often first make sure that everyone is "on message" and agrees to the outcomes and principles of a project.

Imagine a Captain ordering soldiers to move out of the relative safety of a ditch or building and risk being shot. There may not be time for the Captain to sit and go over the moral principles involved, weigh up the relative risks of the strategy or tactics before they are overrun or lose an advantage.

Of course in business the urgencies are usually about commercial outcomes and this is a core difference in the leadership style that is most effective in each situation. There will be situations that lie between the two.

Imagine a group of medical workers faced with a patient who needs urgent treatment to survive. It is hard to imagine a 'co-operative decision making' style working here if they have not already agreed principles and accountabilities.

SO WHAT?

The style of language being used by leaders in an organisation can be radically different depending on the context. It can also indicate the culture, command structure, decision making processes, confidences, and a range of interpersonal, often unspoken, dependencies/structures.

G Fear

Fear is also a driver of language. Think about what style of language might be used based on the level of risk – likelihood of something happening and the hazard – the damage if it did.

It seems that each situation can be evaluated in terms of when to give it attention and how much attention; so the most effective style of leadership and group structure may change.

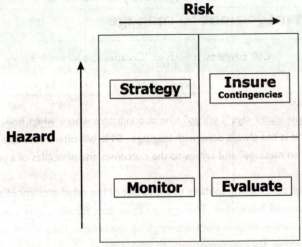

Figure 39 Risk Vs Hazard

Decision making and levels of commitment gives us clues to the group's maturity and fear factors.

To help in this I have constructed a table of language styles used in commitments, see Table 5 'Commitment Levels'. The top level shows a high level of commitment, custody, responsibility taking and culpability. Knowing how committed everyone is provides us with a great deal of control and informs our confidence that we can progress OR that more work needs to be done in cultivating support and commitment.

Commitment generates power by allowing people to rely on others and to offer their own matching commitments.

Level	Said	Interpretation	Possible Responses
1	I am now	I am	Let's go, me too, that's the deal
2	I am going to now	I may start in a minute	Let's go
3	I am going to then	Something else is more important right now	What would make it more likely to happen?
4	I am going to	When I feel more like it	OK, let's set a date
5	I will	I am almost sure I will, sometime	When?
6	I might	I might not	What would cause you to commit?
7	I want	I don't think I will or something is stopping me	What stands in the way right now?
8	I must	I don't want to	Do you want to?
9	I've got to	I don't think I can	What do you need to make it possible?
10	I know I've got to	I don't want to	What is it that discourages you?
11	I understand	I am not saying I agree or disagree	Do you agree?

Table 5 Levels of Commitment in Language

Table 6 has example commitments in negotiations.

Said	Interpretation	Challenge
We would find it extremely difficult to meet that deadline	Not impossible	In an extreme situation what would be the earliest?
Our production line is not set to cope with this requirement	It can be changed, it will cost more or take longer	What would we have to do?
I am not empowered to negotiate this price	See someone else, my boss for instance	Who can help us?
It is not our normal practice to negotiate bulk	I don't know how to do this	OK, we could make some suggestions, tell us more about your systems
Our company never negotiates on price	We negotiate on everything else	What latitude is there in other ways?
We can discuss that point	It's negotiable but deal with my priorities first	Fine, I'll make a note to come back to it before dd/mm/yy
We are not prepared to discuss that at this stage	We want something else first	So what do we need to do first?
We never admit liability	How much do you want to go away?	How much have you dealt with this in the past?
We could not produce that quantity in that time	I may be prepared to negotiate price, delivery, quality, future price etc	What can be done, by when?
It's not our policy to give discounts, but even if we did they would not be as large as 10%	You might get a discount near 10%	What's the best you can offer?
Our price for that quantity is x	For a different quantity there is a different price	What other packages/price/quantities do you offer?
These are our standard contract terms	Please accept them or it will cause me a lot of work	In what circumstances do you vary from the standard?
That is an extremely reasonable price	You might get more if you push	OK, so we are close, we just need the last details

Table 6 Commitment Examples in Negotiation Signalling

The following tables show the underlying structure of language distortion from Neuro Linguistic Programming (Bandler and Grinder ibid).

Distortions

Said	Challenge
I **can't**...	What would happen if you did...
I'm...**because** you're...	How do I make you...If I were not... you would not be...?
This is the right way/thing	For whom? Who says so?
I **know** what is right for...	How do you know that?
He...me	How specifically did he...you?
They don't...	Who doesn't?
I'm (afraid)	Of what are you (afraid)?
My...**doesn't**...	How do you want...to...?
I **never**...	Never? Have you ever?

Table 7 Distortion Structure

Said	Challenge
I can't change supplier.	What would happen if you did change supplier?
I'm wary because you're rushing.	So, if I slowed down you would be more comfortable?
Taking time is the right thing to do.	For whom? In what circumstances is it better to move quickly?
I know what is right for my company.	How did you get to know that?
Your people annoy me.	How specifically do they annoy you?
They don't listen.	Who doesn't?
I am worried about going ahead.	What worries you exactly?
My boss doesn't respect me.	For what would you like him/her to re-spect you and how would they show it?
I never change suppliers.	Never? Have you ever? Even in personal life (your gas supplier?) Then, "What made you make that change?"

Table 8 Distortion Examples

H Influence

It seems very useful to know how committed or uncommitted someone may be, the next thing is to know how to use that and how do we persuade and encourage, especially in fear-laden situations. Here are a few ideas.

Exercise 'IS'

This exercise can increase your ability to be open about how others might view things. It is often difficult at first to do without the word 'is.' Even when writing this heading, so convinced was I of the value of this exercise I first wrote it as follows:

This exercise will increase your ability to be open about how others might view things.

Although I am sure it will, by using the word can, I may appear less confident or less arrogant, depending on the reader's view. Whatever else it does, dropping absolute language allows more discussion and persuades others that we are listening. If you don't want any confusion and you want to dictate instructions to someone then you would probably use 'is, will, must, can't, never' etc.

'IS'
So to increase the range of possibility in negotiating a change in others we can focus on both our language and voice.

This deceptively simple exercise means practising conversation without saying the word 'is'. This causes a radical shift in how you appear to others in terms of your reasonableness.

It also causes us to work harder at meanings and the acceptance of possibilities. Conversely if we are trying to close down possibility we can consciously increase the number of 'is's in our assumptive statements; see next section.

Assumptive Statements

Using 'throw away' lines and moving on quickly is a really simple and obvious trick, yet it seems to work so well when done expertly and simply.

"Since this is the first time we have met it is important that we take time to understand how this meeting will be conducted. So a few rules, if I may..."

What assumptions are in this statement?

1   The other person was aware it was a formal meeting.

2   The speaker can decide what is important without checking with the listener.

3   The listener has time to spend on the subject.

4   The listener is at all interested in how to conduct the meeting - he has not necessarily agreed to attend.

5   That rules are needed for the protocol of a meeting.

6   The listener understands English.

7   The listener has any time at all.

8   The listener has no other more important issues.

9   The listener knows anything about why they are meeting before they talk about how to meet.

I am sure you can add a few and it can be fun to think of more unusual assumptions – **"The listener is human, not an alien."**

Clearly, even without the more extreme examples, the speaker is being manipulative, consciously or not, and we need to avoid this style if possible and to be aware that this may be an important place to put a 'Check-in' statement.
Check-in – A counter to assumptive statements
A check-in is an interrupt that causes people to question an assertion.

In the case above it might go like this:

"I agree that time is important, we have limited time; it may be quite short indeed. I suggest we take 1 minute to set rules and then progress quickly to content."

Clearly one could take this too far and a 'dog fight' could ensue. In my experience one can only helpfully use 'check-in' once per subject, after that it becomes pedantic - too: specific, slow and unhelpful.

5.2 Code For Survival and Sources of Power
For a full treatise on power sources see 'Power Plays' (Quick 1985)

In the world of physics, power is defined as how much energy is exerted at what rate. This is a good clue about how to notice the real power in a group; to notice what/who holds or changes the direction and with what energy at what speed. Who decides the priority and urgency of an activity. What is the source and in what direction, at what rate and energy does action happen?

> ## Who decides on the priority and urgency of an activity?

Culturally an organisation may often be driven by the perception that there is a lack of resources, they are scarcity driven. They operate a 'Restraint System.' Alternatively organisations can be driven by the clarity of leadership - decisiveness or 'System Decision.' These are not two ends of a continuum but rather two separate continua.

Restraint based (Scarcity model)
Poor to Rich

Decision based (Abundance model)
Confusion to Clarity

Restraint Driven (RD) Versus Decision Maker (DM)

RD systems tend to be more neurotic or fearful or both. The decision maker has been trained or decided to be, consultative; to go with the majority forces. In a **DM** system there will be a few or one person who has custody of decisions and makes them confidently (**DM**c) or arrogantly (**DM**a).

In Chapter 2 we saw how you can infer who are the drivers and restrainers in a situation. To know the relative weight/influence of these you will need to watch where the high energy **DM** time goes. If the **DM** refers often to the **RD**s during items of weight, you will know that it is an **RD** power system. If the **DM** does not, and decisions are made with minimal or no reference then clearly the power system is **DM** and the **DM** represents power. Be careful because some high power **DM**s will feign an **RD** system to control negotiations. As in "I only wish I could compromise but my accountant would object."

Sources of Power (Quick 1985)

Source	Example
1. Position	Job Description
2. Personal	Self Belief
3. Autocratic	Coercive / Threatening
4. Assigned / Delegated	From the Boss (es)
5. Associative	Friend of Power
6. Competence	Achievements /Historical & Skills
7. Resources	Owner of resource
8. Alliance	Coalitions
9. Charismatic / Visionary	Sparking interest
10. Reward	Money / Promotion / Interest support
11. Professional	Relevant qualification / Recognition
12. Availability	Opportunity by right time / place

Table 9 Sources of Power 'Power Systems' - Thomas Quick

I use a slightly different system from 'Quick' although many of my terms can be mapped one to one onto his system. It is not important to decide which is the most useful or accurate system, it may be personally easier for some to use one or other system. However, since I am more familiar with my own system I will use it to comment briefly on each.

Sources of Power (used in the Scanner system)

	Scanner	Approx. Thomas Quick equivalents
A	Expert	Competence
B	Historical	Competence
C	Intellectual	?
D	Moral	?
E	Organisational Structure	Position & Availability
F	Personal	Charismatic / Visionary
G	Physical	?
H	Positional	Positional
I	Referential - Relationships - influence	Associative

Table 10 Scanner Sources of Power

A Expert

Because a person has the most experience in a situation they tend to be able to sway groups on the subject. Sometimes this means change is slow. If the expert is in some way wrong and they refuse to accept it, then their influence is likely to be inappropriate.

B Historical

People who have succeeded in the past tend to derive confidence from it, which is influential and others who know of their success may also have an increased confidence in them.

C Intellectual

Those who are able to grasp the relevant issues will be influential but those who can sound intelligent are also often influential even though they have no better insights – see Personal Power.

D Moral

Those who use the moral argument, "We should do this", can have a great deal of influence even in otherwise self interested groups. The pattern Persecutor, Rescuer, Victim is often used to great effect. (See over)

In the illustration below three people enter into a classic Persecutor, Rescuer, Victim trap. This process is from Transactional Analysis (TA TODAY); illustrating how Victims and Persecutors are sometimes created by the arrival of a Rescuer, when, in reality, no victim or persecutor previously existed.

Take a situation in which some feedback has been requested that turns out to be a little hard to take. Person A – Ann, asks person B - Brian, for feedback on some work Ann did. Just as Brian starts to give the requested feedback, person C – Chris arrives on the scene.

Chris feels Brian is being too critical so Chris rescues Ann by attacking Brian; e.g "Hey Brian, that is a bit strong."

The Choice Moment

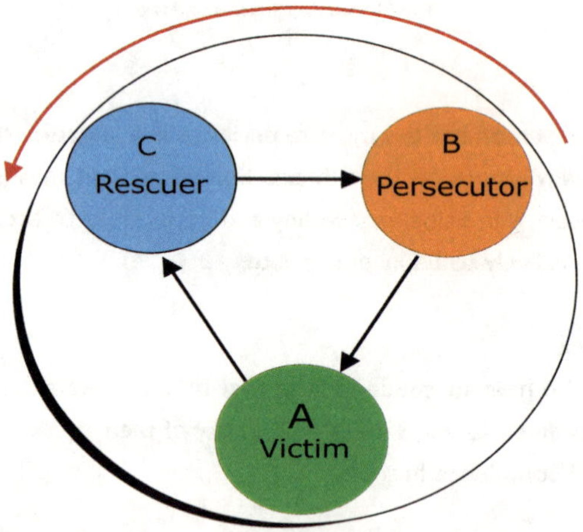

Figure 40 Transactional Analysis

Ann now has a choice, she can fall into the role of Victim and allow Chris to rescue her or she might explain that she asked Brian for feedback and is happy with his honesty.

Another choice is for Ann to defend Brian by remonstrating with Chris; e.g "Hang on Chris, I asked Brian for that feedback, you have misunderstood."

The roles are now flipped over so that **Ann** has become the Rescuer, putting **Chris** in the role of Persecutor and **Brian** in the role of Victim.

It can go around yet again. If Brian objects to being cast as Victim and asserts his rights to defend himself. "No that's not fair, Ann; Chris didn't know you asked me first, from what he has seen it must have appeared a bit too strong." Now Chris is cast as Victim etc. When one becomes aware of this process it sometimes seems amusing, like a farce.

The process starts when someone feels they need to rescue someone. They feel the person is less capable at that moment to defend themselves and in effect this is a very dominating and debilitating attitude in business. Clearly there are situations and clear relationships when people need and/or ask for help.

However, Scanners need to resist the temptation to rescue unless it is an intentional inappropriate interrupt as described in Chapter 2. At the choice moment above if the Scanner wanted to interrupt they might say, "Ann, what do you think about what Brian is saying?"

It is difficult for Ann to play Victim now since she asked for the feedback in the first place. The useful response from Ann might be:

"I wanted an honest opinion, it feels a bit hard to take, but I asked Brian for his honest feedback." Turning to Brian, "It is a little hard to take Brian, can you explain it again, perhaps in private?"

E   Organisational Structure
A person can refer to the way the organisation is structured and how it works in order to influence a decision. "In this organisation I am the only one who would suffer the consequences of this being done badly or well, the client will be calling me for explanations." "It is my department that will have to process whatever system we agree upon."

F   Personal
Often called gravitas this relates to a person's ability to appear authoritative and/or argue their case with good social skills and demeanour.

G Physical

A person's physical attributes can contribute to their influencing skills. There was some untested research in the 70s that suggested height was related to income in American men. Tony Robbins, a motivational speaker of some renown, has many skills and a lot to offer in motivation and life skills; his physical presence, being tall and fit, adds to his personal credibility even if we don't want it to be a factor.

H Positional

A person's job title and their objectives give them the right to assert their authority to decide inside the confines of the position. If one is the manager of distribution, one expects to be intimately involved in any negotiations to change distributor. Changing the objectives of one's department is a matter for consultation for everyone affected.

I Referential - Relationships - Influence

There tends to be an unofficial network in all organisations. It is often a way to get things done quickly and effectively. By building an understanding with colleagues I can pre-empt problems, ask for help, patch over one-off resource shortages, understand where my decisions might affect others. In addition, if others know that someone has the ear of the CEO, perhaps on the golf course or even by living 'next door' to them, there is likely to be a perception of power, even when the CEO has professionally separated personal from business discussions.

Several research projects show that when we understand a group, even in some unrelated way, we are more tolerant in interpreting their actions; being 'in the know' can be a significant source of power or breed resentment.

As a Scanner we pick up on which power systems are being used by whom and those that succeed most in the organisation. This tells us a lot about the company, which argument is likely to appeal to them most, which person at the negotiating table is likely to sway a decision.

It also tells us a lot about the personal power structure of the Decision Maker. E.g, if the DM goes against the prevailing power structure and yet still gets their way, they clearly have a great deal of personal power.

Scanner is complex, even this element of power system analysis deserves its own book. Each system deserves study and practice so that when we let go and do the work we can call on them with confidence.

5.3 Ranking, Put Ups, Shut Ups and Put Downs

I am, We are, They are
(Putting others down to make ourselves more acceptable/ important)

We vs Non We
Having built on the power systems it is easy to see how ranking in organisations exists and can be read: as the team arrives, whose time is most important, who has the final word, who arrives when.

Often DMs (decision makers) will arrive late, the implication being that their time is so precious that they have to make the most of it by being sure everyone else is present before they arrive, which means they don't end up waiting for someone else. If they arrive early you may notice that they attract a zone of calm around them that, if there is a culture of support, will mean people will sit near them for referential power.

If the culture is one of blame, people may prefer to sit further away from the DM. It is as if they feel they can hide if there is any blame flying around.

A subtle but secure means of understanding unspoken ranking is to notice how they refer to each other. How generous are they with the other person's actions. How they 'decline the adjective', see Table 11 'Declining the adjective'. A friend's or power colleague's actions may be judged fairly, assuming they had good intentions. A disliked colleague may be judged more harshly.

Declining the Adjective

I	You/ Power Friend	They/Powerless/ Disliked
...use my money wisely	...could be more generous	...are mean
...make mistakes	...are a mistake maker	...cannot be trusted
...have a pleasant appearance	...are not really handsome	...are ugly

Table 11 Declining the Adjective

Tribes

Are they 'IN' or 'OUT' of the group tribal rituals. A lot of research has been carried out on groups or tribes, perhaps because it lends itself so easily to the classic scientific study. Desmond Morris has written a very accessible book called 'Tribes', and there is the research of P.Zimbardo (1973) – Prisoners and Warders, in which he arbitrarily assigned volunteers the role of Warder or Prisoner in a simulation conducted in a prison. The research showed that groups adopt roles quickly and some behaviour was unacceptable.

It seems we can form close affiliations, even giving over some of our moral and ethical decisions to the group. In a business group there are usually several group affiliations and very complex, even hierarchical loyalties. Noticing these is simply a matter of observation. Are they taking sides based on e.g,

Age	Power
Attractiveness	Religion
Company position	Self interest (a group in itself)
Nationality	Sex
Outcome desired	Social affiliation
Outside interests	Wealth
Proximity (Parochial – the people [closest to me/like me] I understand better)	

I am sure everyone can add to this list. Since humans are social animals it may even be a deep need to be associated. If a person has such a need and finds it difficult to be accepted then they may tend to feel insecure, even lack easy attachment (Bowlby 1997), Ainsworth (1969,1978). Such people will be seeking assurances, see Typologies Chapter 6.

> **If a person has a badge, real or conceptual, it seems they form an allegiance based on it and this effect may be deeply rooted in our psyche.**
>
> C. Edwards

Summary of Chapter 5

The Use of Language (and creation of Coherent Self)

Organising coping and power systems

Right or wrong, power systems exist. Our task is to understand them for our client's benefit inside an ethical system.

Power is achieved and displayed in several ways:

Language
Competence, breadth of use
Power talking
Getting action by analysing group signals
Understanding and checking interpretations
Leaders and Referents
Speech emphasis phrasing – soma content
Risk styles (fear)
Commitment hierarchy
Power sources
Restraint Driven vs Decision Maker (DMc or DMa)
Ranking
Declining the reference (I, YOU, THEY)
Head tilting
Arrogance and confidence

And we have hardly mentioned money?!

Part 3
Models, Tools and Sources for Analysis of Intending Personality – Inferred Behaviour

Purpose
To explain how it is possible to differentiate between the sources of behaviour eg, personality type, developmental experience and personal choices, so that the Scanner can construct appropriate interventions, hypotheses and analyses.

A chic type, a rough type, an odd type
- but never a stereotype.

JEAN-MICHEL JARRE

STYLE, TYPOLOGIES

Chapter 6

STYLE, TYPOLOGIES

PURPOSE

To free resources in the Scanner's mind by clarifying the genetic sources of behaviour and those created by the culture of the subject(s) so that more time and energy can be used for what is left and specific to the person.

OUTCOMES

On completion of this chapter the reader will be able to:

1   Describe three common thinking structure continuums
2   State one of your own style preferences
3   Give an example of how communication can break down between two extremes of style

METHOD

An explanation of the process of evaluation of person type and some examples of common typing (typologies) chosen for their usefulness in scanning.

6.1 Typologies

For hundreds of years, e.g Galen (c.AD129 – c.AD 216), people have been defining people types. I heard a joker say, **"There are two kinds of people in this world; those who think there two kinds of people and those who do not."**

More serious research accelerated during the end of the second world war; now there are hundreds of quality researches, data and theory. How do we come to be an individual human? How do we come to exist?

> **Knowing about certain ways of classifying behaviour helps us to differentiate between what might be innate, learned, cultural and affected.**

Starting at the basics and although there is a lot of debate about Freud, I reproduce here, as an example, a basic Freudian view of the structure of the development of the infant.

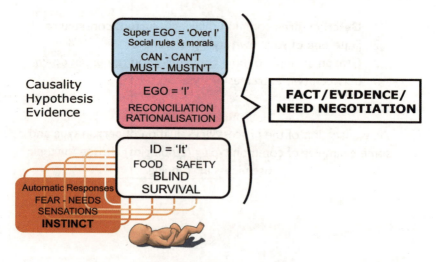

Figure 41 Freud, Ego Development

Basic instincts, reactions to loud sounds, falling backwards, develop in their complexity, application and interaction with the actual environment of the infant to produce programmes of response. Nature interacts with nurture to produce a unique individual.

In the next table I have listed the drivers from a foetus of 27 weeks (line 1) to a baby of a few days old (line 2). Basic genetically driven behaviours develop into successful strategies based on trial, success, error/modification. These behaviours become more sophisticated as the infant applies them to its social context and develop into what Freud called "Super Ego" (line 3). Now the child is an aware social creature, able to interact and make proactive decisions, based on its preferences, habits, abilities and context, about what behaviour to use.

Line	Source	Drivers	Examples
3	Reasoning and Planning	Personal Interest Drivers Source of the 'Over I' or Super Ego	Moral Focus (self, family, tribe) Serial, Parallel
2	Developing Interaction in Social Context	Social Drivers - Coping strategies Source of the 'I' or Ego	Anxious, Secure, Demonstrative, Shy, Angry, Demanding
1	Genetic Survival Programmes	Basic Genetic Drivers Source of the 'It' or ID. Food/Drink/Survival/Fear Contact (Innate fears - large dark shapes and loud noises)	Fear/Need Intravert / Extrovert, Stable/Neurotic, Psychotic

Table 12 Early Drivers

The interaction between our conscious thinking and understanding, and our instinctual – pre-built reactions is complex and dealt with in several other books, e.g Emotional Intelligence (1996), The Biological Basis of Individual Behaviour (1972). See also 'Spreading activation – Appendix 3'

Figure 41 overleaf gives an idea of the complexity.

Rational/Emotional Response System

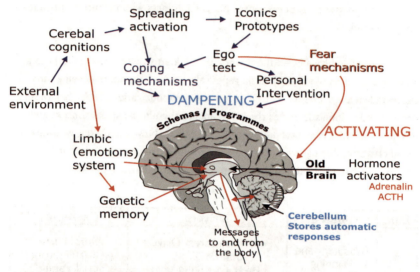

Figure 42 Conceptual Map of Rational Intervention in the Emotional Response System and Processes of Perception of Threat (Edwards 1997)

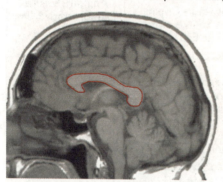

Figure 42b MRI Image of the Centre of a Brain
(Shows Right Hemisphere)

This MRI image of a brain shows that the sections dealing with each part of a reaction are clearly differentiated. Yet how they interact is complex. In the centre, outlined in red, is a section through the corpus callosum where it joins left and right hemispheres. It fans out from here into both hemispheres like the wings of a bird perched in the middle of the brain.

It is a surprise that we are not more surprised by our own actions. Our limbic system, an area that reacts to our perceptions of emotion producing stimuli like threats and attractions, seems almost to connect our five senses to our action response before we have time to consciously know what is going on.

We make a first pass judgement of the appropriate emotional responses through the perigenual cingulate but still need to decide what to do about it. On some occasions a considered or conscious response would be too slow to save us from imminent danger.

Research suggests that our body will prepare for fight or flight on seeing something that suggests there is a predator present, even before the sight has been properly processed in our visual cortex. So before an image of, say, a tiger is formed and arrived at our brain to signal 'Tiger', our perceptions have put together the clues from the environment and we 'feel' scared before we know about what it is that we are scared. It is arguable that, this is another example of the idea of signal anxiety, Chapter 3, Section 4.1, this time working for us positively and it is clearly very useful for survival.

This ability to put together clues and to sense the truth of a situation is a powerful skill. I suspect most animals of any complexity have the same ability. However, we flood our perceptions with irrelevances, ill-perceived threats and imagined intentions. So one of the crucial skills of a Scanner is to **BE QUIET**, so that they are able to access and use clues and really listen. See the exercise called

Leaders and people who resolve things for action sometimes begin conversations with "I don't know". Followers who find it difficult to achieve goals tend to end conversations with "I don't know".

(There are exceptions)

'The Brick', which helps us to create mental quiet.
The beginning of wisdom is listening. Simple words, but how do we really listen?

There is a complex interaction between reactive brain and deciding/thinking brain that begins to produce rules, even before birth and accelerates after birth as the infant begins to interact with a close environment. It accelerates again as the young child becomes aware of its social context and the moral expectations of that context. At first these are about turn taking, sharing or keeping strategies, playing nicely with the other children, doing well for your role model, significant care takers and groups.

A complex enough world of which formal religions, clubs and groups (scouts, school, temples, family events) try to make sense. Just as the growing child makes sense of friendships, moralities and loyalties, a tidal wave of hormonal changes crashes on their perceptual shore.

Sex

Then everything gets a new spin again. The adult sex drive enters the child's world at puberty. How does the child and their sense of self value fare when they find they are desiring/chasing or being desired/chased. The sex 'monkey' climbs on the back and drives the pubescent boy often half crazed with hormonal drives and moral prohibition. The young girl is driven, often ill prepared, into the adult world as her body changes and these changes are there for all to notice; friend, relation, stranger. This time can be rewarding, fulfilling or scarring or all of these. Cultural expectations set up prohibitions and cause a schism, (tension between what the child desires and what it believes is **proper**, ie, acceptable to those to whom it looks for guidance) in the developing child, often pushing desires underground to fester.

The way each person behaves in the presence of others - confident, shy, deferring, embarrassed - may be driven by how well they coped in those early years.

SO WHAT?

Observing and noticing how our clients /participants behave in terms of desire, dependence, risk and exposure can help us to understand why someone is e.g, aggressive one minute and sheepish the next. It can help us to choose the type of negotiator that is likely to get the best outcome. Even attributes we might normally consider irrelevant to the task; Tall/Short, Male/Female, Well presented/Scruffy, Sexually attractive/Dowdy. No person is right or wrong and if we have no choice, which is often the case, at least we can help the client by reducing the effects of the behavioural reaction they are likely to get and the causes.

To sum up typology: I believe that it is possible to take ANY aspect of our experiencing and construct a plausible set of types from it. Currently there are some reputable and useful typologies with associated questionnaires that purport to give us insight into how we are likely to react in given circumstances. I have found them educational and useful in helping people to differentiate between their social/cultural influences, their physiological/predetermined preferences in behaviour, their coping and habit systems and finally, most importantly, where they still have choice about how to react.

Questionnaires you might like to explore for educational purposes are: Myers-Briggs, Peter Honey (Thinking Styles), Drivers, LIFO, FIRO. There are very many questionnaires and the Oxford Psychology Press among others can source questionnaire information.

Current child development research suggests that some basic thinking drivers are decided at conception and some adaptive thinking is formed around the mid 20 weeks of gestation. If this is so, it might seem depressing that our personalities are formed to an extent even before birth. The levels of background neural energy, connectivity and lability (the speed at which our nerve cells recover from firing so that they can fire again), seem to be decided by the time we are born. These things determine whether our background energy is high, low, changeable or stable.

Someone with low energy levels and fast recovering neurons may have too many options to handle all coming to their attention as they speak. They may find it hard to decide or settle on a single course of action. They might be labelled neurotic, yet we can see that this person would be an asset if all the options in a given situation needed to be listed. With high energy, low lability, the person may look decisive and calm. In fact they may be trying to control the information so that they can deal with it.

I am aware that this may seem contradictory but high background energy states in the brain cause the person to want to slow down the input to reduce the arousal. They may seem quieter because of this. Conversely, a low level of background energy may cause the person to want to arouse their brain with outside data; causing them to seem extroverted or perhaps trivial. Valuing both gives a business more options and more flexibility.

Coping
However, from the first social efforts we learn to reduce the unwanted effects of any extremes; introverts make an effort to be gregarious and extroverts to look reliable and mature. The reality of course is that neither is more mature, sensible,

incorrect or correct; they just are what they are. Initial meetings, however, are often full of first impression errors and we all know that. So by finding acceptable ways to engage with people we build coping strategies. "I am excited to see you" becomes "I am pleased to meet you". "What?" becomes "I am pleased to meet you".

So in the end the introvert and the extrovert appear the same to the casual observer. To the Scanner there is much greater depth. They will increase the rate of idea presentation in a seemingly innocent series of stories about irrelevant things. The introvert will become uncomfortable and the extrovert excited.

There are hundreds of scales on which one can be measured and I discover new ones almost every day. Hero to Servant, Controlling to Avoiding, Controlling to Accommodating, Difference to Grouping. As an example here are a few, how we discover them and what we do with them.

META PROGRAMMES

Meta Programmes - Examples

Scale	What you might notice	What you can sometimes do
Active - Theoretical	Sit them down, see how comfortable they are, if they want to know what to do they may be activists, if they want to know what it means, they may be theoretical.	Activists will need to have regular breaks and changes or they will become morose. Theoreticians will need to understand the context and what model it fits.
Towards - Away	The language will be about finding, moving towards something or letting go / rejecting.	Away from people will want to free up their concerns. Towards people will want to know that the future is attractive.
Similar - Different	When options are being discussed the 'similar' person may point out what the options have in common as in "They both/all." A 'Difference' noticer will see the contrasts.	Match their preference in analysis style to build confidence in you. Go from that to joint outcomes. Ask "So now we know how to complete that, is the next project clear?"
Visual / Auditory - Kinaesthetic	See eye access, also their language will predominate in the preferred mode.	Match to get agreement and mismatch if you need to exclude them.
Experience - Process	Experiences will pepper the descriptions or they will only describe sequences of events without colour, sound or feelings.	Match for rapport. Experiencing people will cope with your language but processing people will be very uncomfortable with any feeling content.

Fact - Idea	Things are or they have a quality.	Both people need to know how much time is available for discussion.
Units - Flow	The world is made up of discrete moments or life is a flow.	As the flow person moves along summarise for the units person.

Table 13 Meta Programmes

In addition there are simplistic ways to scale expected reaction styles:

Excitable	1	2	3	4	5	Dull
Respectful	1	2	3	4	5	Casual
Definition	1	2	3	4	5	Freedom
Money	1	2	3	4	5	Interest
Service	1	2	3	4	5	Self

At some point we need a book covering the hundreds of these 'meta programmes', groupings of programmes that drive our behaviour.

We are creating a web page inside www.realise.org & www.acceleratedcoach.com with some of the meta programmes and archetypes and invite the reader to submit their own to us at admin@realise.org. If we can put them on the site we will accredit the sender.

We find out what is in the person by matching for rapport, mismatching for control/exclusion and we infer these 'meta programmes'; programmes that inform, direct actions/beliefs.

The reader might have concerns about the act of mismatching. If a person is dominating unfairly or someone is insensitive to others' time or space needs and we are tasked with, say, chairing a board meeting, we need to have skills to subtly but decisively move on. By moving in and out of match we can send clear and polite messages to get access to their attention systems. E.g. Passionate people often start down a track and lose pace with others. This can be wonderful and empowering, causing the others to increase their energy. Sometimes it goes on and leaves others behind, the passionate person wrapped in their passion can be briefly brought back to the group with a gentle mismatch.

By 'Matching' and then 'Pacing' a person we can get alongside them to encourage them to move on, to make a clear point for discussion/agreement. If they do not move on and time is pressing we need to pace them out of their mode so that they connect with their share of space, time and attention naturally.

Pacing is about keeping step with someone until you are both, e.g. talking in similar mode at a similar pace, taking turns fairly and easily. We then 'lead' them to a new place by pushing against the rapport proximity – starting to change the pace subtly or introducing a different criterion. See example 12 Table 14 Discussion Levels re-visited.

Of course this is only one of several possible ways the conversation could have developed. However, notice how often now the thought matches what is said.

What other ways could both have matched or paced each other? Language, speed, volume, lilt of speech, body language, specific word choice, etc.

Example 12 Match Pace Lead

Person A Says (and thinks)	A Hears...	B Hears...	Person B Says (and thinks)
We need to talk about promotions. **(Who should we promote?)**	⟹	**How should we decide who should be promoted?**	⟱
⟱	**How will we know how we will be doing it?**	⟸	To what outcome? (What do you need?)
I need to know how it will work. **(What is the best process?)**		**I want to be safe.**	
	When?		I understand. Do you want to do that now or tomorrow? *Checking conceptual space.*
Tomorrow at 10? **(Tomorrow at 10?)**	⟹	**That would be safe for me.**	⟱

			Great, is there anything else to talk about tomorrow? **(Is that your real concern?)**
	I want to be safe.	⟵	
No that's all. Do you think we can solve it tomorrow? **(Am I going to be safe?)**	⟹	I want to be safe.	⬇
⬇	Are you ok with this?	⟵	I'm sure we can, we both want to get an agreement, so I'm looking forward to it. Are we done for now? **(Are we done for now?)**
Yes great, we'll get it done tomorrow. **(Looking forward to tomorrow.)**	⟹	Looking forward to tomorrow.	OK, bye. **(Me too.)**

Table 14 Discussion Levels revisited

6.2 Maturity

Analysing the maturity of a person's behaviour is one of the easiest ways to start to get insight into a person's motivations and commitments. When you see someone change the way they are expressing themselves, imagine the example on the next page:

Example	Imagined Age	What it means
"You're not going to get away with this".	1 - 6	"I want to smack you."
"Where were you?"	7	"I'm not playing with you if you don't care about me?"
"I will not allow that."	9	"No fair"
"I will have to think about that before I comment."	11	"I don't know if I want to."
"What is the best solution?"	Teen	"I don't know, can we just do something?"
"I believe we should do X, ok?"	Late Teen	"I want to do this."

Table 15 Maturity Levels

SO WHAT?

This is not infallible or definitive, it does help us to begin to evaluate, with other evidence how deeply ingrained the behaviour might be and to think about what kind of language would be most helpful in response. Imagine a child is saying the thing in the last column but they have a loaded gun in their hands. What could you say in response?

I have seen CEO's of some very large organisations screaming at their employees and some middle managers actually stamping their feet in rage. It is clear that our childhood behaviours sometimes persist and are sometimes barely translated to make them more acceptable.

Selman (1997) analysed children's friendship-making behaviour, compared it with other child development psychologists like Piaget and produced the following table:

Selman's Friendship Maturity

Stage (yoa)	Individual	Friendship	Peer Group	Physical / Cognitive	Level
0 (3-7)	Physical Entity	Momentary Physical Playmate	Physical Connections	Intuitive Pre-Operational	1A/ 1B
1 (4-9)	Intentional Subject	One-way Assistance	Unilateral Relations	Transitional Pre-Concrete Operational	2A
2 (6-9)	Intro-spective Self	Fair Weather Co-operation	Bilateral Partnerships	Consolidated Concrete Operational	2B
3 (9-15)	Stable Personality	Intimate-mutual Sharing	Homogenous Community	Transitional Concrete/ Formal Operational	3A
4 (12+)	Complex Self Analysis	Autonomous Inter-dependence	Pluralistic Organisation	Consolidated Formal Operational	3B

Table 16 Friendship Maturity

I observed a particular manager in a meeting jumping up and down with clenched fist, spitting as he was shouting with a red face, saying he was not excitable! Many of us conceal our driving emotions even from ourselves so a Scanner needs to be very careful not to point out behaviour, if the clients have concealed it from themselves, unless you have their expressed permission to do so (in some cases this might be best done from inside a steel cage).

"Don't teach Giraffes to whistle"

Giraffe Ethics

To prevent frustration for the client and to keep people focused on the client's instructions there is a general principle of engagement, "do not teach someone who has not asked to be taught". For example:

1   The Giraffe may not have the physical mechanisms needed for whistling and may not have the desire to whistle.

2   More importantly, you might really annoy the Giraffe.

Figure 43 Giraffe Ethics

It is difficult; especially if we notice mechanisms/behaviours that are causing problems with which we could provide assistance. Yet sometimes it is clear that we are not correctly placed to have our view on some things accepted, either with good grace or at all. When and if to speak is often a cultural choice.

6.3 Archetypes

For the purpose of this book I will define archetype as a definition of a typical sort of person, the architecture of personality. E.g, Military - to mean decisive, structured, strong; Ballerina – to mean graceful, ethereal, professional; Wizard – mysterious, knowledgeable, arcane, etc. In Jungian psychology, an inherited pattern of thought or symbolic imagery derived from the past collective experience and present in the individual unconscious.

There are hundreds of archetypes. Attaching an archetype to a person on first seeing them is very common and can be very wrong. Within a few minutes however, we seem to pick out those parts of a person that confirm which set or collection of certain sorts of personalities they have in their psyche. We seem to have a sort of arsenal of potential styles upon which we can call. Knowing about a person's general types can help to understand: how they process some of the information and situations they face, what are the limitations of their thinking, what types of solutions they might prefer etc.

Listening Styles

The Emotional listener may only want to know how what you are saying is a threat or support, so if you want a proper unbiased evaluation of ideas, you will need to contract with them first. E.g, "We don't know how this will affect your department. I would like to discuss it in general and then evaluate the effect on your department of the different options."

For each of the listening types below, think about how you might break through their expectations in order to get access to real thinking.

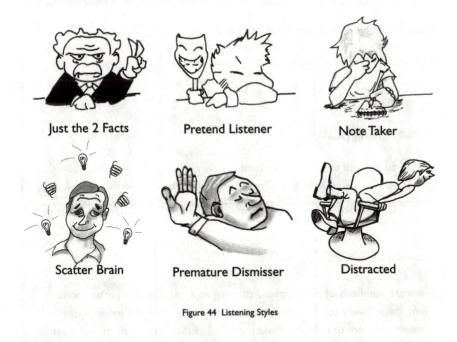

Just the 2 Facts   Pretend Listener   Note Taker

Scatter Brain   Premature Dismisser   Distracted

Figure 44 Listening Styles

In the late nineteen sixties a social class shift was in progress. The advent of computing, the contraceptive pill, the threat of nuclear annihilation all conspired to cause a sense that the desire for personal freedom was more achievable. People wanted to challenge authority and social repressions. There are challenges in every generation, this one seemed to be about class. There were many comical confrontations as the rich and poor, the comfortable and the rebel came closer in income and power. Taxes that attacked the 'ruling' classes like death duties took their toll on the underpinning power structure of old money.

It is easier to be an anarchist when you have little to lose.

Have a look at the cartoon below for fun.

1 New face   2 Introductions   3 Get to know you

4 Tell you about me   5 Brag - Bravado   6 Tell you what to do

7 Tell you how to run your life   **8 Get blown off**

Figure 45 Social Expectations

Increasing levels of access to the higher decision making levels in companies for technically skilled specialists broke through some of the older closed boardrooms. As a computer analyst I was thrust into boardrooms in my early 20s. Unused to etiquette or forms of address, I made frequent style mistakes (which of course I enjoyed immensely).

The power of technical knowledge was unmistakable and people in my position found doors open that had been closed for generations. I was amazed at the complete lack of common sense in most companies run by 'old money' and spent many profitable years engaged in turning unprofitable companies into stable ones with very simple processes.

SO WHAT?

Business often seems to run on personality rather than rationality and people can have very unique and different reasons to run a business or to agree to a price. Often when I arrived at a company it was failing to deliver, trading in a bankrupt condition or delivering problematic solutions. The ethos of the board in these cases was inevitably patronising in a well-meaning way. They often saw themselves as heroes giving the client what, in their wisdom, the client needed, not always what they wanted or could afford.

Example 13 Motivation Differences - Paradigms

A client company was on the verge of declaring bankruptcy nearly every year, but found a new investor each time. They would close down and reopen on the same premises, with the same staff and products a day later. We sorted out their finances and products, reduced losses and streamlined processes. As I left they gave me a dinner and after the port I asked what had kept them going for so long.

The MD said, "While our doors were open to business we were supporting several families in this community and we have seen children born who would not have existed otherwise." It was never about profitability or even sustainability, he felt responsible for his group of local people as if he were still the land owner his ancestors had been.

He seemed to have a sense of mission. However a lot of large and small companies and investors had lost money. In a strange turnabout he seemed more Robin Hood than missionary.

Personally, I felt humbled by this. The "so what" I got from that experience is that - **"THERE IS NO UNIVERSAL HUMAN TRUTH"**. Each person constructs their lives to suit their view of the world. As Scanners we need to get insight into how they construe their worlds if we are to succeed in persuading them or indeed in persuading ourselves. (See Watzlawick, 1993, Schema Chapter 3)

Sources for Archetypes
Myers-Briggs MBTI, Adlerian fear types, Jungian archetypes, Peter Honey's Learning Styles, Drivers, Right Brain Behaviour, Kelly's behaviour Types, Neurology as a Source of Behaviour - Skinner.

Examples of Archetypes
Hero, Angel, Dark woman, Tempter, Failure, Wizard/Witch, Sage/Guru, Idiot, Fool, Leader/ King/Queen, Earth mother, Priest/ess, Devil, God, Optimist, Naïve clever, Naïve dim, Wise

person, Seer, Rich, Poor, Easy going, Neurotic, Artisan, Artist, Old money, New money, Crude, Adroit, Civilised, Natural. I am sure you can go on with this list.

SO WHAT?

Some people adopt an archetype or two and play out of that. If they do, we can trap them in a decision. They often find that they cannot escape without changing their identity. People often make decisions against logic to save them from that kind of wrench, which challenges their beliefs and habitual behaviour and thinking patterns.

Passive Aggressive

The following definition is pragmatic, that is, it is more concerned with practical application than pure definition and is not exactly the same as that in the authoritative books, 'Games People Play', 'TA Today'. For me a 'passive aggressive' is a person who believes: the world is often unjust; they can see it clearly and are always just themselves.

They tend to believe they will fail but the struggle makes them heroic. When a group succeeds at something they begin to praise everyone in the hope it will cause others to praise them so that they can humbly deny any major role but graciously accept the view that they are "a little wonder." The common phrase from them at this point would start, "Oh no, I just..." playing down their part.

Example 14 Passive Aggressive

A passive aggressive will spend ages telling you of their exploits and hard work. If you show them how it could be done with less effort, they are affronted.

> In the Hitch-hiker's Guide to the Galaxy (Adams 1992), Arthur Dent saves everyone's lives and as he is praised says, **"Well, it was nothing really."**
>
> Zefod replies, **"Oh was it?"** Zefod has not played the game, he has accepted at face value that Arthur's contribution was nothing.
>
> Arthur, now feeling cheated, tries to recapture the original praise but no-one seems interested.

You will find you cannot criticise this person; they make no definitive assertions on which you can focus. A classic passive aggressive sentence from them starts:

"I would have thought you would have wanted to..."
e.g, **"wait longer."**

Notice the layers behind which they hide:

Passive Aggressive Constructs

What is said	Back Down Contingency
I would have,	I didn't.
thought,	I'm not saying I am sure, so don't blame me if it doesn't work out.
you would have,	Doesn't mean I would or you should have or anyone else could have.
wanted to ...	There may be a reason you didn't but you might have wanted to do it, did you?

Table 17 Passive Aggressive Constructs

An alternative and assertive statement might be:

"I think we can wait a bit longer."

If your client prefers aggression they might say,

"You should wait."

In training we talk about the masks people wear, there are usually at least three (1-Me, the result of my developed systems of coping working as a coherent persona, 2- What I want to be and 3-What I want you to see me as) sometimes many more. The next illustration is a representation of the assertiveness choices as masks.

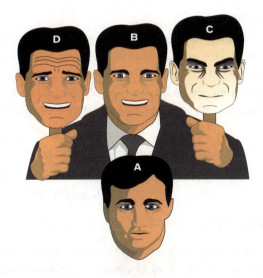

Figure 46 Aggressive Assertive non Assertive

As we observe people we can often see the original face A in the illustration struggling to get through. When the world does not do what we want, then Mask C might pop up to confront the world. If the reaction to Mask C is rejection, Mask D may defensively appear and backtrack on any aggression. This gives some respite but there is a residual feeling of loss of control.

As a result the person is continually forming compromise presentations, our socialised personae compete for the lead position in our dealings. These personae will sense the environment and choose what is the most effective combination of response for that situation. In times of uncertainty and stress the result is an ambiguous appearance – Mask B. It is often easy to pick up on 3 levels of mask and people may have many more.

A warning

Archetypes are fast ways to get a head start on the process of insight but they can be misleading. We need lots of supporting evidence and to be prepared to change our expectations as the continuing evidence gives us more clues.

CONTROL TYPES (Attachment)

From a very early age we learn how to gain control of outcomes. The work of Ainsworth & Wittig (1969) gave us a plausible way to analyse choices in behaviour of infants. John Bowlby (1997) called them attachments and Ainsworth cited three types, one secure (type B) and two types of insecure attachment. Main and Solomon (1986 & 1990) later identified a third form of insecure attachment, disorganised:

Type A	Type B	Type C	Type D
Avoidant	Secure	Ambivalent Resistant	Disorganised

Some books label the types differently e.g, calling Secure Type A

It seems that most of us can behave in these 'insecure' ways from time to time, Ainsworth and others are attempting to understand how to define any preference for type. Those with a preference for a type will revert under stress or perhaps even habitually, in one or a combination of these ways, while those who tend towards secure reactions will tend to be able to remain calm and to act rather than react.

Knowing about these types can help us to understand how a person makes decisions about resisting or joining a group or how they might adopt an idea/ideology.

Avoiders *find attachment reminds them of insecurity so they avoid the opportunity.*

Ambivalents *seek comfort and or/to blame someone for their fears of abandonment.*

Disorganised *appears chaotic and gives rise to affirmation seeking behaviour (Be my friend).*

At time of going to press there was a useful description on web site: http://www.gpc.edu/~bbrown/psyc1501/childdev/attachinvent.htm

In Situations of Risk:

If someone is either quiet or making short comments and then stepping out of a conversation appearing to communicate "Do what you want, it's none of my business", this would be suggesting that they might have a default behaviour preference of avoidant.

If someone is trying to take control, becoming dominant (often called Alpha behaviour) or holding a view for one side of the group despite evidence, they are likely to prefer Resistant behaviours.

By trying to curry favour or taking whichever side is most conciliatory or by looking bewildered about which side to choose or changing their minds back and forth often, they might be showing a preference for a Disorganised attachment style.

SO WHAT?

Once a person gives away their style we can be sure to avoid feeding their anxiety. We can form close relationships with a Secure. An Avoidant will prefer if we keep to business (see Cold in Typologies). And an Ambivalent needs consistency in the delivery of messages. So don't teach them until they ask and always find the positive in everything they say. With the Disorganised stay calm, simple and clear. Try not to change anything you have said and if you have to make a change, give them plenty of warning and reasons.

While this is not a book about self help, it is worth mentioning that even becoming aware that these behaviours are options or choices, we may start to gain more control over how we behave. For the Scanner in a short time scale noticing others' preferences helps us to design approaches that will reduce stress for them.

I have explained the idea quickly and indeed each category is better defined in Ainsworth's / Main's work. Many other researchers have gone on to differentiate even more usefully; avoidant - insecure, resistant-clinging, disorganised – disorientated, etc. Some have made it a lot easier to remember and use by constructing everyday examples, see over.

The three types are described in **Alan Schoonmaker's** book (1975) on sales technique in a triad of:

Detached   **Dominant**   **Dependent**

He argues that each is an extreme and most people use some combination of these. We try to absent ourselves completely from any desire or connection to the person's emotions/needs, or we seek to dominate them, or we depend on their goodwill toward us.

As Scanners we need to know how to respond in terms of their intent to control themselves internally and in relation to ideas. So we use the terms:

Cold   **Hard**   **Warm/Soft**

A Cold person presents no connection (as Alan describes it they have detached from others) no warmth comes through. The pack Alpha (Hard) is the individual who wants every other animal in the pack to do as it is told. The warm person is all over us as we enter a room to ensure we will not hurt them or do something against their interests.

Handshakes

If the person is unaware of it they can often unwittingly show which approach they prefer. **Even at an initial meeting we can tell a lot from the handshakes.**

Cold   **Hard**   **Warm**

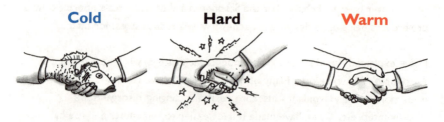

Figure 47 Handshake Typology

Who is which in the next picture?

Figure 48 Handshake Personality

The harder person is not always the upper hand. Imagine what it would feel like for each person and you will realise that the person on the right is putting energy into the handshake causing the other person to bend their wrist into a weaker angle. However, if the person on the right were leaning back and using a limp handshake they may be signalling detachedness or lack of respect. Again it is important to triangulate – to use information from several sources in order to properly interpret.

SO WHAT?
Cold
On the left of Figure 47 is the cold or 'wet fish' handshake; they will be smart and clean so that no-one can criticise them, that would be too personal. Their office will be clinical and their work methodical. When you offer a compliment, address things and achievements, nothing personal. If you keep cool long enough they will warm up to you. In the boardroom they will respond to ideas and processes not feelings, justice not complaints. They will work with people who have undeniable authority and avoid the risky, "silly" people.

Hard
In the middle is the hard handshake that establishes physical superiority at the outset. Do not get into a competition with this person, no—one can win it. Stand your ground. They will dress powerfully and stand erect, everything about them will be impressive; their car, their office, even their children. Interestingly their

spouse is often not as impressive. Do not agree for the sake of it, do not attempt to dominate them or submit, they will eventually accept you as an equal.

Warm/Soft

On the right of Figure 47 is a warm handshake, someone who 'Slimes us'. They will be chaotic in their organisation of their desks, clothes and life in general because they are more interested in the 'Soft' issues. Generally they will want to please people and many people find it easier to deal with them.

(Young monkeys given a soft woolly surrogate mother were found to be less anxious than those who had a cold wire surrogate.)

It is easy to mistake someone dressed for business as hard or cold. Look at the picture to the left.

Although he seems smart, his general appearance might be described as dishevelled. No extreme Cold would wear a coat that was so casual or trousers that crumpled at the ankle. Also the smile is too accommodating and Warm for a Hard or a Cold.

Remember that this model is not subtle and it is only likely to be of use in the first few seconds or minutes of meeting someone. Although we need to continue to be aware of their preferences in how they would like us to relate (or to not relate) to them, there will be a need for further rapport systems as we get more comfortable and these may be more subtle.

The next system I will cover is how we organise our thinking.

Figure 49 Warm Man - Istockphotos Inc.

6.4 Serial - Parallel/Network

Serial thinking and Parallel thinking are both available to us all otherwise we could not walk and talk. According to the work of Oliver Sacks (1985 and others) there is a right/left brain difference in processing. There is a real experiential difference in thinking styles evidenced by how we are able to think through one idea at a time, link by link to a conclusion and how we can sense the general area in which the answers might be by inference using almost unrelated clues to point us in the "right" direction. The first we will call Serial thinking and the second Parallel or Network.

Some people have suggested that when we use these two processes equally well, we are much more creative and capable.

SO WHAT?
If we are working with someone who has excellent serial skills but has not had much parallel thinking practice, we have to go from A to Z in a straight line, showing how we have made our conclusions and giving supporting evidence.

In groups where serial people seem to be slowing things down, the parallel thinkers are often quite uncomfortable with progress asking "What is their problem?".

Equally a predominantly parallel thinker may hold things up because they have forgotten to complete a task, to sign the document, or explain how they chose a solution, going off on to other ideas, other business opportunities.

We need to collect all the ideas and agreements and just before we finish, list them out, stopping on each one to get a yes or no. This process is very helpful for all parties and is part of a formal board meeting process anyway.

6.5 Drivers and Fears

In 1977 I wrote about the two predominant types of prospect that sales people face in decision making.

Feeling   Thinking

In dealing with a Feeler we need to listen to what they want and respect that even if they say left they may mean right.

A Thinker will be proud that they are not swayed by emotion, so if you notice they are being illogical, you may want to think twice before you point it out (see Giraffes).

In difficult situations, especially in the face of an outburst of emotion directed at your client or even you, there are four stages that will calm things down.

1. Accept   2. Validate   3. Support   4. Act

A simple mnemonic to remember is **AdViSA** (sorry about the spelling)

1. Accept - Don't Deny their emotion even if you deny their conclusion(s) or their facts.
Allow the person to own the emotion, **don't deny** that they have it. You may not be able to accept their evidence or their desired actions but you must accept that they are experiencing an emotion if they are (so long as it is not harmful to you).

"I accept that you believe you are being ignored."

2. Validate
Give the person assurance that they are not rejected, you are still interested in their case.

"I am sure that if I felt I was being ignored I would be saying the same things (feeling the same way), I believe we can sort this out together."

3. Support

Make a suggestion of what you think might be helpful; an action.

"I suggest we take a moment to listen to your concerns to be clear about them before we go any further?"

4. Act

Ensure you take note, even document their concerns and follow up on anything you have agreed and that you check back that the action has had the expected outcome. If you don't and it goes wrong, the client may never trust you again.

If the conversation moves into imagined motives ask if you can discuss that once you have a corrective process in place. Then make sure you return to discuss it however briefly.

6.5.1 Drivers

From Transactional analysis Michael Reddy (no reference) talks about Transitional Drivers. These are underlying beliefs that we adopt in early life about how best to succeed in the world, .

They are unconscious internal pressures that makes us do things certain ways, e.g with speed, perfection, little emotion etc. If we overdo them, use them in inappropriate situations, they become unhelpful. If others understand our drivers they can easily manipulate us by appealing to them. If a manager is aware of his/her staff's drivers she/he can choose tasks to suit them. However, they tend to satisfy our inner perceived needs rather than the needs of the actual events. These represent a classification of the main drivers:

Be Perfect - Hurry Up - Please People - Be Strong - Try Hard
Imagine a child laying toy blocks out to make a house or a bridge, how would each style behave:

Be Perfect
"I'll have to square up the blocks exactly" (as if perfect accuracy was important)

Hurry Up

"I'll have to see how fast I can build the column" (as if speed was important)

Please People

"I'll look around to see who is watching me" (as if the approval of others is the most important thing)

Be Strong

"I'll sit on the floor rather than sit at a table" (as if the discomfort gives the task added merit)

Try Hard

"I'll try it out horizontally first" (as if the extra effort was worthwhile on its own)

In a meeting it is possible to observe decisions and rewards based on these beliefs rather than business objectives. This is not wrong but it provides us with significant insight to how a decision might be made and influenced.

6.5.2 Fears

We are born with a fear of large dark shadows and loud bangs. We also have an inbuilt 'away from' pain instinct and a 'toward' pleasure instinct. We learn to build more specific fears and desires based on these and sometimes it produces very different reactions in people. Someone who has been punished for failing, even once, if it was embarrassing enough, will fear failing and this will drive their negotiations.

Imagine a child scolded for being 'dirty', perhaps they soiled their bed or clothes. If the child does not deal with the memory well, they may be driven by the fear of discovery for many years. In negotiation they may feel the deal is too flaky, too mucky, not clean enough and become fearful.

Imagine a child is rewarded for being clean. They may desire cleanliness and strive for good deals that are clear, becoming eager and excited.

SO WHAT?

When we notice the basis for decision in the individual we can steer the conversation to accommodate their comfort position to achieve agreement.

IMAGINATION

If we hear a sound late at night and we fear being burgled, we might start to add elements to the sounds in our minds and convince ourselves we are hearing voices and things being searched. Yet, if we go downstairs we find a hungry cat rummaging through the bin. Many of us can remember as a child, the sound of aliens or the latest horror story villain coming up the stairs. At that age a blanket pulled over our head is an impenetrable shield against all such ills.

> **"The safest thing is to imagine the worst, then you are prepared."**
>
> **Vs**
>
> **"You can't live in fear, it makes you fail."**

In the boardroom, if the Directors are uncomfortable they may imagine that staying as they are (even if they are losing market share at an alarming rate) will somehow make everything right – a security blanket.

Scanners often make people feel uncomfortable long enough to get them to choose an 'away from' strategy. In our "Cat" example (see Exemplars/Schemas Chapter 3) the client starts to realise that their fear is controlling them. This state is undesirable and they find another way to assess whether it is a cat or a professional assassin. When they realise it is definitely the cat and go downstairs to put the cat out, they celebrate their courage. Now the risk is that of being afraid of failing. Sometimes it is someone horrible downstairs, be careful not fearful, you have **choice**. The idea that we can choose at times when we may feel we can not is very powerful for our clients.

In the same way, when person A doubts the motives of person B, person A is likely to imagine the worst in their fear. So to create a positive exchange, we have a saying, that is not unique to Scanner:

> **Be 'Hard on the subject and Soft on the person'**
> (Remember that sometimes the rule is 'Break the rule')

At the end of the day everyone is responsible for their own outcomes. Scanners are not expected to decide what a person will do, we are expected to interpret what they want. In addition we provide information relevant to the desired outcome that will help to achieve the best possible outcome we can for everyone.

Journey vs Destination It is easy to notice this difference once you become aware of it. Someone who wants their everyday life to be of a certain quality and strives to maintain this, will often find outcomes irrelevant. If they have any measures at all that exist in a single moment in time.

Sales Managers and Accountants might find it very frustrating to have to deal with a 'journey person' since they spend a great deal of energy setting goals and meeting them. Extremes on both sides often find the other incomprehensible. We can help by showing that a single moment measure is a check-point on a journey. This translates one system into the units of the other. How would you persuade a goal based person of the usefulness of a journey based person's ideas?

Instructor/leader, Instructed/follower It seems that if we have no measurable goals, those with measurable goals appear more persuasive. People seem to gravitate to certainty and hard measures have the capability of providing the illusion, if not the fact, of a definite outcome. As usual, the most effective people seem able to make the best of both. Further, those without hard goals seem to be susceptible to being taken along with the flow of those who have them. Clearly this can be a force for good or evil. It means that many forgo their free choice as they give in to this 'certainty'.

SO WHAT?
Once we understand this mechanism we can understand who is who in a group. If it is important to gain real commitment from everyone in the group, we can balance strong goals with strong vision to give the followers a choice. This will not annoy the leaders if it is seen to augment their thinking.

Multi Schemas/Flexible vs Limited Schemas/Inflexible
In most situations it is clear very quickly who is confident enough to examine alternatives and who finds it difficult.

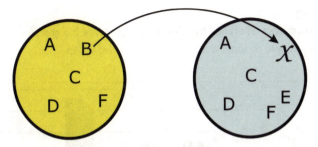

Person 1 tries to communicate something to Person 2, e.g, that they want to give them a gift, say, buy them a tie. Person 1 has a belief, 'B' - a schema that we might call a 'free gift.' It will hold links to friendship value, generosity etc.

Person 2 does not have a schema 'free gift'. The nearest they have is 'X' - 'There are no free lunches' so they suspect the gift and even feel manipulated. We can deal with this by helping both sides understand that if they want to communicate they have to create extensions to their schemas, admit possibilities outside their experience.

Living/driven vs Existing/waiting These are extremes and the driven person can be too much for some people to take after a while. People who have achieved their goals and settled, perhaps with a great income, partner, children, house, friends, can eventually find they have lost their motivation. For some, eventually, there are no goals worth achieving.

"When Alexander saw the breadth of his domain, he wept for there were no more worlds to conquer."

It is hard to tell which is which until you get them on a subject close to their passions. To warm up a 'waiting' group find their passion. As one, driven, CEO said, **"A way of life is not always a way of being."**

In Summary:

People are motivated differently by different things. Here is a graph of the results of asking two people to score their motivation on five topics:

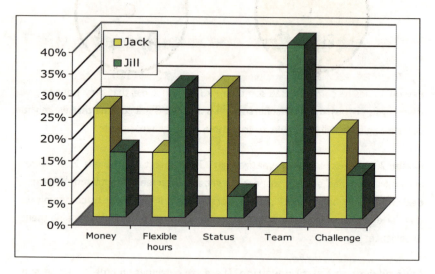

Figure 51 Motivation

Taking out **Jill's** answers and putting all the columns together makes it look like the spines on a key. So we can see the key that would unlock their motivation.

Jack's answers demonstrate the key to his motivation is very different to Jill's. Scanners and Managers need to be aware of the needs of the individual.

Figure 52 Keys to Motivation

The test of a first-rate intelligence is the ability to hold two opposed ideas in the mind at the same time, and still retain the ability to function.

F. SCOTT FITZGERALD
THE CRACK-UP, 1936

THINKING STYLES

Chapter 7

THINKING STYLES (COGNITIVE)

Purpose

To provide additional descriptions and explanations of terms, models and meanings contained in this book.

Outcomes

On completion of this chapter the reader will be able to:

1 Describe a number of processes and models used in scanning
2 Describe some of the ways people can hide their motivations
3 Describe with insight how a defence can become an attack
4 Turn some language tricks of others into an advantage

Method

Providing ideas and examples.

7.1 Paradigm (Cognitive Schemas)

So far we have looked at behaviour and the sources of behaviour. You might characterise these as 'knee jerk' actions. However, when we work with people we need to take into account what some call the universal spark or their knowledge of self. Often referred to cynically by some managers as, "Bloody minded ability to not do what you expect of them."

The average professional may have spent decades perfecting a front and they may play that persona expertly. Faced with a difficult decision or a 'double bind' (see next page) they are quite capable of surprising everyone even themselves. As Clint Eastwood explained in one of his spaghetti westerns, it isn't the professional; it is the lucky amateur that will get you.

We are dealing with a chaotic system, luckily it is not actually chaos, there are patterns and only our pattern finding brain can deal with these efficiently. So notice what you notice and then ask, "What does that mean?" Wait for any understandings from your networking brain and then evaluate them with your linear mind asking, "Is that my mind providing meaning that is not present or is that really there?"

7.2 Paradigms, Models, Sequences

After a few minutes with someone you can pick out their paradigms, just listen for absolutes (Modal operators of necessity in NLP).

An example, **"You can't go around expecting people to owe you a living."**

They may have a genuine lack of understanding of how you are able to do, what they think, you can't do.

There are several paradigms that we call 'coded models' about how the world is organised, that are likely to be present here:
"You can't..."

They may truly believe that they can say something to you that will restrict you in your actions. The source of this belief may be cultural, experience, job position or a genuine lack of understanding of how you are able to do what they think you can't do.

"...expecting people to..."
It seems here that they believe that it is not possible for you to have expectations of others in a specific area. Equally, because they use a specific situation – "...owe you a living." It tells us that they may accept that there are areas in which you <u>**can**</u> have expectations of others.

Making the whole assertion may mean:
1   These areas of expectation are clear to them and are universal rules.
2   There are rules with which you must comply.
3   You have to earn a living.
4   You cannot expect gifts.
5   People can have erroneous expectations.

There may be many more coded in this simple sentence. Listening like this for coded beliefs enables us to work out the stand point of our clients and to phrase our interventions inside their expectations, thus making them more readily understood and increasing compliance.

7.2.1   Traps and Trapping for Analysis (Double Binds) "Doing it means not doing it"

A "Double Bind" is a way of pitting the client's logic against itself where there may be a contradiction. Imagine a manager who believes she/he faces facts and is strong. In order to delegate can they be personally strong enough to say they want help?

Equally we can use it more subtly. Eg, in order to get a resolution or to redress an out-of-balance power system with a client we can use a statement to which the client agrees and yet it contradicts itself and resolves in a decision in the client's mind.

Example 15 Taking Responsibility

C "Cliff, you know what's best to do in these situations."

S "Well I believe what's best in this specific situation is for you to decide what's best."

C "Sorry Cliff I disagree."

S "With what?

C "I think you are best positioned to decide."

S "OK, well my decision is that I want you to decide what to do."

C "OK, so if I agree to go ahead, that's all right with you?"

S "Absolutely, so long as that is your decision I am happy to support it."

C "So you think we should go ahead?"

S "If that's your decision, I do very much."

The reader may find this supercilious or just arrogant; in this instance it was vital that the CEO was clear that this was his decision and previous attempts to explain that had failed. His confidence in me was, in this instance, over extended and he was failing to take personal responsibility.

Cognitive Contradictions

It seems that the 'unconscious' has the capacity to hold two or more contradictory beliefs without having to reconcile them. This is a very useful thing for us to be able to do. If we were faced with a contradiction and had no choice but to reconcile it, then we would be unable to sleep or to get on with the everyday essential activities to sustain life.

While coaching a senior manager many years ago, 1981, he made a classic statement of inner conflict. He had lost someone close to him and he had been religiously devout for many years. So what do you think may have caused him to make the statement in the next example?

Example 16 Deleted Logic - Replay

C "I don't believe in God, he is a swine."

S " I see, you think that God is a swine and does not exist, is that right?"

After a moment's thought the client's anger disappeard, he seemed sad and said,

C   "No, I just **don't** understand."

This was a step towards reconciliation for him and it took him many months to work through the emotion. However, it was quite all right for him to hold the contradiction for a while and he needed to do that. If he had not been ready to process it, he would have answered inside the belief instead eg, "Yes, how could he let so many bad things happen?"

So what does this mean for a Scanner. The client and person being observed may not always make sense to you. They will make perfect sense to themselves; so our task is to understand their rules. Sometimes just stating the words back to them can open up more possibility, Rogers (2003).

I was asked to observe the following conversation.

Example 17 No Time to Get it Right

The client found she was having trouble motivating her staff.
C= Client, **M**=Manager, **S**=Scanner.

C "I want you to take on XYZ in your portfolio."
M "You know I am already overloaded, XYZ is a massive account. Let me assign it to 'n' he is ready for a challenge and I will support him."
C "No, XYZ is a vital account and I want you on it."
M "So what can I drop or pass on to you or 'n'
C "Currently nothing. I will try to get you some help next month but I can't promise anything."

M "I just don't have the time right now with recruitment and being a person down in head count."

C "You will have to make the time, I have to come in early and stay late to get things done, so will you."

M was now rising from her chair, obviously intent on saying something that would be career challenging for one of them.

S To M - "Can I check that you want M to work longer hours like you?"

C "Yes."

S "Are you happy working longer hours?"

C "No, but it has to be done."

S "Can I check to see if M has any alternatives to doing something you don't like doing?"

C nodded

M "I could ask two other clients - ABC and DEF if they would be happy with 'n' for a month so long as they have access to me if they need me, or even if they just feel they need me. Then I could ask HR to process some of the recruitment data for me and put off the interviews until the following week. I could then crack the back of the XYZ initial negotiations and have time to introduce 'n' for everyday events, putting in an escalation procedure in the Service Level Agreement.

C looked surprised and asked

C "Can you guarantee you will be on top of everything?"

M "More than I would if I had everything to do on my own."

C "OK you have a point, I want weekly reports."

M "Oh no, now you are adding even more work load."

S "How detailed, what form, what would be the seriousness of missing a report?"

C "A five-minute telephone call Thursday or Friday every week and I must have that. I want to be able to report on what is going on. I can't have a director asking me what is happening and not know."

Example 17 No Time to Get it Right (continued)

M "Oh, I thought you wanted a standard written project report, a call is fine and I can send you a proper report if there is an incident or an exception. I would do that anyway."

C "Great, that is terrific."

M "Do you want help with any of your work?"

C "No I am fine."

The Scanner kept quiet at this point, **not** teaching giraffes (see giraffe ethics in the previous chapter). What do you think would have happened the scanner had said, "So, you are saying you are unhappy with working overtime and you don't want any help?"

Think about it carefully before you answer, the clues are all there.

7.3 Mental Capacities

In the 1930s 13 psychologists went into a conference to decide on a definition of IQ and they came out with 13 different definitions. Useful?

Intelligence is not a single thing, here are a few of the forms of intelligence:

Academic
IQ (a measurable ability to recognise patterns and to perform everyday basic processes)
Leadership
Psychomotor *Mind moving body* - physical co-ordination
Social
Creative
Emotional
Artistic

In addition we generally assess people on their ability to keep up with us, to allow for possibility, and to have a breadth of models and understanding to call upon in the conversation.

So when we are working with someone we can pretty much work out where are their problems and success by the areas they find difficult or easy. If they have communication issues with us, it is likely that will be a sore point for them because they will have that issue elsewhere as well.

If they use a single 'killer' phrase or phrasing they are likely to be limited in defensive scope.

Magic Mirror

For instance a manager who constantly says, "What do you mean?" Whenever she/he doesn't understand AND whenever he/she doesn't want to reply, will likely have no other defence, especially if you mirror that back to them.

Eg "When you say, 'What do you mean?', what do you mean?"

Having used this on a persistent offender, I can say it is the 'doomsday' weapon of conversational manipulation. Not only was this particular manager dumfounded and extremely helpful after that, He was also unable to function in the position from that day on. He could not use this dumb defence with such confidence and had no other 'tricks' upon which to fall back. I call this the doomsday weapon because, once used, it has no way back and it can destroy not only their power with you but also your relationship with them and their power with everyone else. It is a last resort.

SO WHAT?

Once you are aware of a linguistic trick, you can be prepared for it and find other ways to get what you need without destroying everything. Instead I could have said, "I understand it doesn't make sense to you, can you help anyway?" **This preserves the 'protective ambiguity' and the irrationality and perhaps the relationship.**

Protective Ambiguity

Having used the term I guess it makes sense to explain it. This is one of the most common forms of linguistic/cognitive/social miss-agreements in use. I pointlessly fought against them during the first few decades of my life and then realised they are part of the normal social world.

I found programming a computer simple compared to understanding everyday social interaction, which is why I made a study of it. I made a great deal of money programming computers and later in life de-programming groups, see W R Bion reference. What most people, probably including you dear reader, take for granted, I sweated over for years until I believe I found the structure and was able to write it down. I hope it is for everyone's benefit and to extend understanding for both practitioner and social structure students.

So what is Protective Ambiguity? It is an intentionally badly constructed communication which may have more than one meaning. Because it is unclear, people are unable to grasp its meaning and are impelled to make an arbitrary or random decision about the meaning. This means it is not possible to criticise the speaker because they can simply assert you misunderstood, even if they know you did not.

1 "I don't know what you feel I thought you might have said."

2 "Yes, I was going to have bought it."

3 I believe the cartoon character Popeye used these eg., "Language is used more for conversing than any other."

Examples:

To create this, we need to make up a phrase asserting something without completion, eg,

"Buses leaving around now..."

And finish it with an unrelated phrase that appears in structure to complete the sentence.

"...might have left wanting."

So we get: "Buses leaving around now, might have left wanting."

You might well ask, "wanting what?" and one feels as if one has missed some previous information. Perhaps someone asked, "Buses should have ticket inspectors, many leave wanting one."

Not common English but had this been said earlier it would make sense of the last statement. However, people use this construction even when there was no previous set-up. Often they have extended an idea or conversation in their thinking and forget that this thinking was never spoken out loud. Some very clever people do it to create insecurity in others.

In our conversations we are hardly ever accurate or precise. Companies spend millions on writing unambiguous contracts and more millions defending their meaning in courts later, as they realise they are being sued for still being ambiguous. In addition to the innate ambiguity, people sometimes intentionally construct it so that, if the other side doesn't like what was said or are using it against us, we can always say,

"That's not what I meant!"

We can then proceed to rewrite the meaning to suit our purpose now that the other side have declared their position. Here is an example of an everyday married couple engaging in this nonsense:

Example 18 Protective Ambiguity

PERSON 1	PERSON 2
Do you like this hat?	Oh! yes.
Can I wear it to the party?	Of course you can.
Yes, but do you think it would be suitable?	I would tell you if I thought it looked silly.

I think it is clear that if 'Person 2' really thought the hat was suitable they would have responded very differently.

Example 18 Protective Ambiguity (continued)

Do you like this hat?	Great!
Can I wear it to the party?	It is just the thing for the party
Yes but do you think it would be suitable?	Just right, I can't imagine anything better

Person 1 is hedging their bets and this is easy to see if the conversation veers off and Person 2 reveals their thinking.

Do you like this hat?	Oh yes.
Can I wear it to the party?	Of course you can.
Veering off Oh! I don't think it is really suitable	No, I was going to say, you can wear it, but there might be a better one for this party.

So we can build ambiguity to protect ourselves or we can just use it carelessly to build insecurity in others, causing them to have to ask for clarity and giving us the upper hand or at least giving us time to work out what we want to say next.

Example 19 Pronoun Misuse

If you think this can only mean one thing, try again. In social interaction the pronoun does not always have to relate to the last noun. So is Mary telling Sue that Jayne

> Here is an extreme example: (Pronoun misuse) Jim tells John:
>
> **Jim** "Mary met Sue and told her that Jayne wanted her to know that she was looking forward to working with her."

wants Mary to know that Jayne wants to work with Mary or for Sue to know that Jayne wants to work with Jayne or Mary? Confused? That's what it is like when socialisers forget communication.

It gets worse. Look what happens when confused John tries to get it clear:

John	"Sorry Jim, are you saying Jayne is looking forward to working with Mary?"
Jim	"No, of course not, she wanted Sue to know that she was looking forward to working with SUE!"
John	"No sorry John, I still don't get it. Mary wanted Sue to know that Mary is looking forward to working with Sue?"
Jim	"Oh don't worry, I just thought you would like to know."
John	"But I still don't know."
Jim	"Yea..., never mind."

Obviously this is extreme and they would probably have worked it out with hand signals. For more on ambiguity see the section on commitment levels under Power in Chapter 5.

Part 4
The Last Word?

Purpose
To remove from the rest of the text and collect together all those interesting parts of the Scanner story that people ask about and so prevent those parts interrupting the flow of the rest of the book.

A man begins cutting
his wisdom teeth the first time he bites off
more than he can chew.

HERB CAEN

WHAT NEXT?

Chapter 8

WHAT NEXT?

Purpose:

To describe the background and sources of Scanner.

Outcomes:

On completion of reading this chapter the reader will be able to:

1 Explain how we are able to address culture imbalances in companies.
2 Describe how Scanner came about historically.
3 Describe how to continue to increase Scanning expertise.

Method

A description of the ethos, reasons for the development, history of Scanner, exercises.

8.1 Beginnings

8.1.1 Cultural Balance

It is worth noting as we go into an organisation that "One chunk leads to another chunk" as Cadbury's said in an advertisement; implying that once you try a chunk of their chocolate you will want another.

This is also true in an organisation that as soon as someone who is unaware of personal prejudice is involved and influential in the recruitment process they will tend to identify with, and give preference to, people who match them or provide a codependent contract with them. Their particular style will become encoded in all the processes. If it is a senior person in HR their prejudices will influence the kind of person who succeeds in the organisation. So one 'low reactor' leads to another and so on.

What I mean by codependence here is that the person senses an unspoken contract of benefit in their interactions with someone. This provides a sense of eg, security, excitement etc.

Example 20 Contracts in Style

A new recruit has an authority issue; they are in awe of authority and defer to anyone in a power position. As the interview progresses the insecure manager feels at ease because none of his/her assertions are contradicted and their assertions may even be extended to bring out added justifications.

M "I think that clarity of concrete, measurable goals and processes is vital to the efficiency of any organisation."

R "I agree and that clarity helps us to deal with any uncertainties in our clients or suppliers."

The manager FEELS comfortable. The next candidate enjoys the manager's assertions, has no issue with authority and perhaps is not aware that anyone else might, so they extend the manager's assertions by questioning and testing. The manager feels: taken to task, her/his values are being threatened and uncomfortable.

Another manager prides him/herself on learning and teaching, meeting the same two candidates they may find the first interesting but unchallenging, while the second was refreshingly honest and they both felt they met and matched a person who was equal in their ability to test thinking. If they continue to be unaware of this mechanism they will pre-sort people coming into the organisation and find they either have no diplomats or no challengers.

The effect of this on the organisation is not felt for some time. At some point catastrophic failure begins with no-one in the company able to reverse it. The company calls for the counter culture consultant, who finds it impossible to carry out the revamping task given, because the whole culture continues to miss the change needed, they continue to support their existing assertions supported by all those in power around them. It is out of line with the current need, but they are like fish who can't see the water in which they are swimming.

So the company fills up with people of a similar nature, rejecting counter culture people. Clearly in terms of flexibility and resilience this is unhealthy for the organisation and correcting it can be a long and difficult task. We need to explain the process to the CEO and, if we can gain their support, we can begin remedial action. Begin by ensuring all interviews, reviews and especially exit interviews are conducted by at least two people who are as different from each other as possible.

> **"An unhealthy Codependancy creeps into our behaviour sometimes, so slowly that, just as fish don't notice the water in which they swim, we take our maladjusted behaviour for granted."**
>
> C Edwards

Neutrality is NOT enough – codependance creeps into our behaviour, it is so insidious that even if someone is committed to being fair they can succumb to it. Providing two opposing styles at interview reduces the risk by at least a half. A Myers-Briggs questionnaire is one way of ensuring people are different although it is not recommended that it is used during the interview on the person being recruited.

Personal note: I happened to notice that I was the only non-blue eyed person in my department and that I was the only one who was not interviewed at the first stage by the (blue eyed) IT manager; who had been on holiday at the time. I found this interesting at age 22 and mentioned it at our departmental meeting over coffee. To their credit the organisation went back over a year of interviews to ensure fairness in their processes. However the results were never published, even internally?

FAQs

What Next?
Scanner Master, the inside story (also in Accelerated Coach). This course pulls together the theories that allow the person to create/generate new models and to contribute to the practice of Scanner. Successful participation in the advanced course qualifies the advanced Scanner for master level membership and support from the Scanner organisation.

8.1.2 How Did Scanner Arrive?

1969 - 1975: I taught myself (with help from a colleague, John Norman) how to program a computer. It had 16K of memory and a massive 5MB of disc storage. Today it would be called a pretty weak calculator. We had to write space efficient code. Over the next 6 years the coding I developed went from detailed code to do really simple jobs really quickly to systems that inferred answers to complex questions including heuristic programming- self teaching programmes; the basis of artificial intelligence. I learned to develop logic and sequences of logic quickly.

1975 - 1981: I moved onto being a business analyst, which meant talking with people who did not understand computers but needed programs to help them. For 6 years I learned how to listen and question and to listen to what they were not saying. The most common specification in those days, the late 1970s, was "Then I want to be able to just press a button and it will do it."

It became apparent that all systems could be coded into 'add, delete, duplicate, modify, calculate, report'. All you had to do was to find out what information they needed, then trace back to find out where it came from and decide how it should be entered into and extracted from the computer. I earned a lot of money for little work but I learned all about how business runs and makes or loses profit. I also learned how people exist in corporate life. I had access from boardroom to post room. I also began to meet real leaders: often they were CEOs, sometimes they were quiet people tucked away, hidden in the process, who loved being able to drive a business but didn't like the spotlight to fall on them – in case they had to join the political arena for which they were often ill equipped.

The back end of this period I worked with several companies on their profitability a sort of company doctor. This job is encompassed by business financial advisors, non-executive directors and chief accountants now. By understanding the real business drivers I was able to notice those that were artificial - ego or selfish faction driven. This gave me tremendous insight into the 'corporate person' and corporate culture.

1981 - 1989: as a tutor in management skills, I learned and taught human systems to new managers and directors. I taught for 30 weeks out of 48 a year, this meant that for most of my mental processing time I was interacting with people whose main task was working with people. I learned about all the approaches, the successes and serious failings. It was confirmed that business is often driven by ego rather than by any greater purpose or logic.

One manager, explained this better, "We work to live, not live to work and if we can make our work part of our life we can enjoy that too." He followed up by saying, "If they are making your life miserable, don't let them." This led to one of our sayings: "If a person upsets you and you stay upset they got you twice. Every time you remember and feel angry, they get you again."

I invested time in a degree in Psychology, much of which was unexpectedly illuminating, from child development to social psychology and social constructivism. I learned about ways of seeing background human interaction that helped or hindered. I learned about the incredible nonsense that survives and flourishes and the pain that we ignore and endure, thinking it is the way it is supposed to be. Good people (essentially everyone) strive to make sense of their lives, to construct a viable life.

> **"If a person upsets you and you stay upset they got you twice.
> Every time you remember and feel angry, they get you again."**
>
> C Edwards

Finally I found the most important message for reconciling people – "If they are doing 'it' to you, someone probably did 'it' to them." There were many lessons, the magic mirror, schema, attachment, transactions, which you can read about in this book.

> **"If they are doing it to you, someone probably did it to them."**
>
> C Edwards

I suggested to the owner of the first UK NLP Schools, Sue Knight that I needed to know the aim of learning. She said "That's true for you." She kept on saying it as I protested and finally I got it. A frustrating and useful message to remember – "Universal truth is rare, mostly truth is about interpretation."

I believe we programme ourselves and much of that programming we take as a universal truth, rather than a personal way of interpreting the world. Perhaps even that is only **my truth**.

It came together
Everything - structures, logic, rationale, psychology, management, people in action - came together in a synthesis (a Gestalt) and the model was clear. We humans devour processes and encode them for later use. We combine and synthesise these into programs that form beliefs, habits, behaviours, paradigms and prejudices. The more options, ways of seeing a situation we have, the more mature, flexible and stronger we become. In our training work we offer access to new ways of thinking.

Every day people add to our list of known schemas. As Scanners, we have built a significant base of possible paradigms to which people, by the time they are around 18, have access. Now we are able to offer a structure to organise schemas and thinking so that people are clear about their thinking, they know what they know. We are also taking the guesswork out of interviewing across the board in busines.

World Peace? (if you want it enough)

Programmes like Scanner have the capacity to help us to reconcile our differences and to join together to make a just world for us, our friends, our perceived enemies and generations to come, by translating, explaining how what we are saying is the same even though it may sometimes sound completely opposite.

We were invited to write a paper for a conference of very learned people on world justice for presentation in Africa. People from every religion, politic and theology shared views, and the shock? Everyone was stalking (talking until they found) the same language. It is our belief that the opportunity for significant justice, joy, friendship and salvation is only a matter of translation. While we are talking we are not killing, so for humanity's sake, let's keep talking.

For a copy of the paper, visit www.realise.org or www.acceleratedcoach.com.

8.1.3 Examples of Scanner Elements

These are some of the things we scan to get information from people.

Era / Age	Attention focus	Attention limits	Language choice But/And
Environmental	Eye access	Financial reserves	History of action
Is/Seems	Maturity	Voice tone	Idea repeats
Processing speed	Repeated actions	Resilience	Skin tone
Tenacity	Vocabulary	Paradigm	Body tone

Table 18 Scan Elements

There are hundreds of ways to get information and the list also includes:

Body Language	Gross and fine
Voice	Speed, accent, volume, vocabulary, rhythm
Other People's Reactions	
Cross Modal Behaviour	Similar acted out beliefs (in more than one part of their behaviour)
Stacks	Conceptual stacks sizes
Extant Tolerance	The number of unresolved ideas they can have in their minds at once

We can always resort to the obvious - ask them about their preferences. There have been many meetings that turned around, producing much more positive progress after the simple question "What would you like to happen?".

As a new manager in a department I always ask each person, "What would you like to keep, what would you like to change". One can't always do what they want but you know where you are starting and what are likely to be the main issues. They don't always tell the truth? Yes I guess so....

Appendices

Appendix 1 - Role Sets

As children we learn coping behaviours, these become complex and inter linked into programs or Role Sets. Role Sets (habituated responses) are often viewed as being the person, rather than their behaviour. It is often very difficult to recognise these or to accept that they are affectations, practised artificial behaviours, because they are so deeply ingrained, let alone get access to the programs and change them.

Role Sets are often useful ways to deal with the world until they drive the direction of the person's life. If we remember they are affectations then we can suspend or delete them to suit our needs. (See also Schema programmes. Chapter 3)

How? If something is going wrong or you feel troubled by how something is playing out, ask what is it about your actions that is supporting your real needs and what you could change to more closely resemble your intention and your character.

Appendix 2 Decision-making Neurons

Our brains are neural networks that have subtle abilities to change. Each time a pathway fires it is more likely to fire the next time. The neurons not only increase and decrease their sensitivity, they are also able to make the decision to fire based on a simple logic. Decisions can be processed in basic ways, e.g., AND, OR, XOR. This is called Boolean logic and is similar to that used in digital electronics. I have attempted an explanation of that below.

Each neuron receives charges from several sources and decide to pass on a charge to hundreds of other cells based on three kinds of criteria.

.AND.	Did I get a charge from both/all sources?
.OR.	Did I get a charge from any of the sources?
.XOR.	Did I get a charge from only one of the sources but not both/all?

So if I use a 1 to stand for a charge and a 0 for no charge, the following table shows how decisions are made. In the results column a 1 means the signal is passed on, a 0 result means it is not:

AND			OR			XOR		
A	**B**	**Result**	**A**	**B**	**Result**	**A**	**B**	**Result**
1	1	1	1	1	1	1	1	0
1	0	0	1	0	1	1	0	1
0	0	0	0	1	1	0	1	1
0	1	0	0	0	0	0	0	0

Table 19 Boolean Logic

Note: There does seem to be a periodicity in the brain, evidence is the ability to wake at an exact time without an alarm clock, musicians who keep perfect time.

Appendix 3 Spreading Activation

In Chapter 3 under "Schema and Schema Programmes" and again under "Word Association" I suggested that people have automatic responses to words and other stimuli. A way of supporting this neurologically is the idea of "Spreading Activation", (Collins & Loftus, 1975). It has been used to describe how the brain links ideas, words etc in a network of relationships.

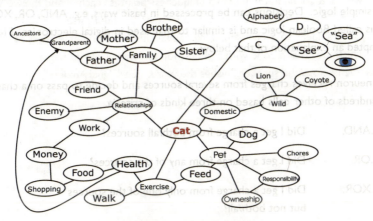

Figure 53 Spreading Activation

As the person hears the word 'Cat' it automatically generates other representations in the brain. Some of these predominate in attention and perhaps with other stimuli – the time of day, the person becomes aware that they need to 'Feed' the 'Cat'. However they also remember that their ageing Grandfather has not been feeling well and '…perhaps they should call him'. The link is so tenuous that they may not even be aware of it. Each set of neurons in this theory have an activation level. Activation is raised by related neurons increasing the energy or prevalence of the idea, each adding weight to the idea. So background worry about 'Grandad', feelings of responsibility and a sense of time passing are already present as this person realises they need to 'take care' of their cat, which means feeding it, worrying that it has the proper 'exercise' / 'food' ratio, which leads to thoughts of 'Health' which adds the final energy to the idea of 'Grandad' to bring him into awareness.

This is a speculative theory but it seems to represent well how we respond, think, remember and forget, it has face value, 'on the face of it', it seems to represent what happens. (McClelland & Rumelhart, 1981) and (Rumelhart et al, 1986) for more reading on the subject.

In addition Marslen-Wilson (1978) described a process called "Parallel Activation" which again demonstrates the relational structure of brain function. As words are spoken the brain is reacting to each sound raising the level of activation of all words with that sound in them until a uniqueness point is reached and the word is identified. This is efficient in time and understanding and it raises the activation level of several ideas so even a sound like "Spike" might be processed first as "Spi.." which means someone with a phobia for spiders is likely to begin to feel uneasy even before the speaker finishes the word. See "Signal Anxiety"

Exercises

The Watch

Next time you find you are anxious, sit somewhere quiet and watch the second hand on your watch go around twice.

If you have a thought, simply promise you will think about that later.

When you finish, notice the difference in your capacity and arousal state.

If you have succeeded in calming your neurons down you will find it gives you more energy and time seems to be slower. This is a perception based on a physiological effect. Your neurons rely on their ability to maintain an electrical difference, a potential. Maintaining the potential during high levels of mental activity for long periods can cause misfiring, slow firing and result in confusion and sluggish decisions. Even a minute of rest can allow your neurons to catch up.

Having mastered the watch we can move onto calm breathing twice a day for five minutes. Sit quietly and as before think of nothing, be a dead brick, have nothing to do, perceive, nothing to which you need to react. Now when you meet the next person, notice how much more you can pick up from them and how much faster.

Mary Ainsworth suggested that we have levels of activation of groups of neurons representing ideas and as these activation levels rise, the ideas compete (my word as interpretation) for our conscious attention. If we are able to put all these back at rest twice a day, it clears the slate, improves the chance of new experience starting at the same point of importance in our minds. The effect is that we make faster, calmer, better assessments of what is going on in front of us.

Eyes - Hyper Input

When you have good quietening skills (See 'The Brick') then practise increasing your attention by being excited about what your audience might say; you will find you are responding to questions and unease in individuals as they sense it themselves, even in a large audience. My personal experience was that I knew the state of everyone in an auditorium of 200 people within seconds of entering the room. It was a surprise to me and too powerful that first time to handle. I found

I had to withdraw, the effect was too shocking. Since that day I have tried to recover the ability slowly to reduce the effect on my neurological system to a level with which I can cope. So far I am back up to (sustainably) 25 and briefly (lasts around 20 seconds) around 100.

Exercise Eyes (seeing the wood for the trees) De-focus

When people realise how much information is available they often ask how they can take it all in. Luckily our brains have a facility to pre-sort information for us but mostly people seem unaware of their capability.

If you can find a safe place with a view that has lots of items in it, a forest or a typical high street shopping centre, walk through it, being very careful to be safe, without focusing on anything and be aware of your surroundings. This is sometimes called defocused seeing. In this effect the mind takes over the conceptual focusing and sorting and you may be amazed at how much information you suddenly start to take in, process and understand. Many martial arts training programmes teach this defocused method.

Figure 54 De-Focus to Scan

The Brick

Find a quiet place where you can look at a brick in a wall. Imagine the history of the brick from the dawn of time, through several suns, to our planet where it sat for millions of years until it was mined, transferred to a factory, moulded, fired, set in a wall with other bricks. See if you can imagine that it has a character (assigning emotion to an object is called anthropomorphising eg., a loved Teddy Bear or car seems to assume a personality) which most people can do with practice. Now, realising that in reality a brick has no emotion, you become aware that if you can imagine emotions in an inanimate object like a brick, how you might see them in others. We can do this even though the emotions may not be there, or misinterpret those emotions that are present. Creating a state of being inert in terms of our prejudices is the state we call, "being a brick". When you are happy with this ask yourself "So what or where is the difference between a "Live Brick" and a "Dead Brick".

Cognitive Dissonance

Normally ideas run around our brains in a pretty orderly fashion, one idea leading to others, leading to yet others in a cascade that produces an idea. When there is nowhere for a signal to go then we sense it as an uneasy feeling of "What next??" This is cognitive dissonance. The signal reaches a dead end with no connections. At this point the brain resorts to either cancelling the thought or to making a new connection. In other words, we decide to forget it or to learn a new thing or a new way. This effect can be created in a person by asking a structurally correct question that in reality has no sensible answer. Or by asking someone to act in a way they have not done before.

As an exercise, we show people how this feels, so they can notice it in others and are not surprised and thrown off if it happens to them in a session.

"I will ask you a question and your task is to not answer the question but to say something that makes sense in the context and is polite."

Then ask a trivial question e.g., "Where did you get that tie?" and tell them that they only win the game when they are unable to answer and they have sensed that feeling of unease. We are given the programme as children, "Answer when you are spoken to". What is the sensation as you go against that programming? Does it feel like you go off the end of a cliff, there is nowhere to go?

This reflects what is actually happening in the brain. Your thoughts literally find nowhere to go and the energy that was flying along the neurons, goes into space. However, the brain will quickly find a route and you learn a new option in thinking. If you pause and focus at that point you can also learn how to deal with that feeling every time from now on. You have the means, an awareness of the sensation and the brain code for generalised, intentional cognitive learning.

Exercise Faces

Adding a mouth seems to change how we perceive the eyes.

With the addition of eyebrows the emotions are changed even exaggerated.

Figure 55 Eye Interpretation (Based on an idea from S Drury)

Exercise Eye Contact

This exercise has been around at least 30 years and helps people to be more comfortable in diplomatic and intimate conversations.

Two people sit comfortably on chairs facing each other with knees touching. Sit straight upright looking directly into each other's eyes. Feet should be directly under knees so that the lower leg is vertical. Place your hands comfortably on your upper thighs.

Sit like this for two minutes without laughing, talking, signalling in any way. Many people find this very difficult at first and once someone starts to laugh it is hard to re-compose the pair.

Animals only look in each other's eyes for specific reasons, eg as a prelude to confrontation, mating or deciding which.

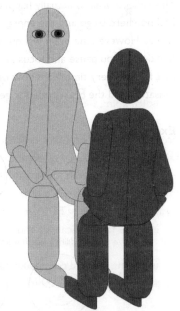

Humans are social animals and we have developed our communication skills using facial expressions; there are six that are pretty universal to all humans. However, not communicating while still staring in the eyes takes us back to the original purpose and civilised people find it hard to deal with this.

Figure 56 Eye to Eye

Once we are comfortable with two minutes we can extend it to four minutes and that should be enough for our purposes as Scanners; we can now hold eye contact comfortably. This will enable us to not back down yet not threaten dominant people if they try to stare us down, nor to make shy people uncomfortable.

Absent Mind, Present Eyes
A word of warning, you can become quite intrusive if you become thoughtful yet you are comfortable with eye contact. You might forget to look away as you think, and people have said it is like you are looking into their soul and reading their minds – when actually you have just remembered a previous part of the conversation that you are trying to integrate into what they have just said, or to get the potatoes on the way home.

Exercise Reverse Anchoring

This process should only be used with a qualified Scanner or master NLP practitioner until you are confident with its use.

In order to re-programme an unhelpful reaction, a schema programme, we need access to the Choice point, see Schema Programmes.

Here is a simple process that enables access. Have the person sit quietly and ask them to describe the sequence of events as they know it. Get as much sensory description as possible; colours, sounds, smells and feelings. Ask them what the feelings remind them of so that you have some real depth of sympathy (normally we aim for empathy – knowing how the other is feeling: here we need sympathy – feeling how the other is feeling). This is quite intimate for the Scanner and some people find it difficult,

Now use some physical continuum, often their arm. With permission put your hand on their arm just below their shoulder and ask them to recall the causal event as in -

S   "Tell me, what happens to start this off?"

Then ask them to describe the events. As they start remove your hand and slowly move it in their sight towards their hand, timing it to arrive as they complete the events. If you misjudge and run out of arm, ask them to put their arm on the table and then move your hand beyond their hand in a straight line along the table.

When they reach the end, go back to the original causal event, touch their arm just below the shoulder as you did before and move it down to the elbow as you ask:

S   "So what is the next smallest sensation you get?"

As they recall information ask them to show you on their arm roughly how far down is each sensation. If they don't understand, take time to explain the whole process again and ask them to use their imagination.

By moving your hand into intervening spaces it is possible to cause the thoughts to change their decision points and to move along old pathways, re-accessing the original programmes so that the client can decide again whether they want that programme as it is or to change it.

Once the client decides which route they want, they have already begun to re-programme it. If they want to cause it to be the preferred route, especially if it is a fast reaction like losing your temper, that they want to stop, we can help them to 'Anchor' the new choice.

Start with your hand at the point on their arm that corresponds to the causal event and get them to fully remember it, using the sights, sounds, tastes, feelings. Now move your hand to their elbow saying something outrageous, here are some examples:

"The queen on the toilet", "Your mother on a Harley", "Mickey Mouse in retirement", "What would it be like to have an eye on your index finger and pick your nose", or make up something specific to them, or get them to make up something. In NLP this is called a 'break state' because it causes the brain to go off in a radiating way from the original thought.

Now move your hand to their hand and get them to recall the desired outcome, what they want to be thinking when 'Jim arrives' (See Schemas).

Finally get them to run the whole thing and ask them to keep running it for a week every morning when they wake and every evening before going to sleep.

If this is not successful there may be an intervening fear of letting go of the old behaviour. If they still want to change, suggest they work with an NLP master on 'Working With Parts' (Sue Knight).

OPCASE® OPerational CASEs (face value)

This questionnaire is an example of a forced choice questionnaire that supports the subject in taking time to evaluate how they deal with the world. It makes the assumption that each of us puts differing levels of energy into, and priorities onto, motivations in seeking satisfaction. This affects how we view possibilities and how we choose to operate.

Eg, a classification or differentiation of the areas on which we concentrate could be:

Internal (personal values based)	**External** (approval of others)
Measurable outcomes	**Life style** (every day satisfying experiences)
Discrete elements (Structured processes)	**Intuitive experiencing**
Variety	**Predictability**

Table 19 Focus of Energy - OPCASE

If this were true for you, what do you think your profile might be in these areas?

It might help to understand how people take value from their efforts and those of others if you assess some of your preferences by completing the questionnaire on our web site.

There are other, more commercially tested questionnaires used by psychologists, personal developers, trainers etc. Some are only available to qualified personnel through official sources like Oxford University Press and OPP. Others are supplied by the designers of the questionnaires and there are many on the internet. Questionnaire examples are: MBTI Myers-Briggs Type Indicator and LIFO (Life Orientations®). Simple examples are: Learning styles (Honey, P), SDI (Strength Deployment Inventory), Drivers (Reddy, M), Team roles (Belbin, M), and Conflict styles (Kilman, T).

A copy of the OPCASE questionnaire can be found at www.realise.org/scanner or www.acceleratedcoach.com/scanner

Neither the author nor his representatives nor agents warrant the predictability of results from OPCASE; it represents face value only. This questionnaire has been designed as a training tool only to show an example of typologies and no value is implied to its use or content in any way.

List of Illustrations

List of Tables

List of Tables (continued)

Examples

Glossary of Terms

Conscious That part of thinking of which the person is aware. Sometimes the term sub-conscious is used to refer to thinking that is not clearly available to the person and not completely unconscious; they are only aware that some thinking is going on but not know the content.

Corpus Callosum The largest white matter structure in the mammalian brain. It consists mostly of contralateral axon projections. It appears as a wide, flat region just ventral (below) the cortex. It is missing in monotremes. It intimately connects the right and left hemispheres of the brain.

Exemplar An instance or representative of a concept; more generally something to be copied or imitated. (Oxford Dictionary of Psychology 2003.) For this context: The minimal conceptual representation of something (C Edwards).

Extants (in this context) Incomplete (unfinished) thoughts that keep some of the mind's attention reserved.

Kinæsthetic Relating to kinæsthesis - the ability to feel movements of the limbs and body.

Lability (in this context) The speed at which our nerve cells recover from firing so that they can fire again.

Neural Placticity The capacity of the nervous system to change its reactivity as the result of successive activations.

Limbic System A set of forebrain structures common to all mammals. It is implicated in the higher integration of visceral, olfactory and somatic information as well as homeostatic responses including fundamental survival behaviors (feeding, mating, emotion). (Carpenter's Human Neuroanatomy)

Psychotic A person suffering from any severe mental disorder in which contact with reality is lost or highly distorted.

Psychoanalysis The process of analysing and attempting to understand a person's set of mental rules and conditions.

Psychotherapy Making changes to mental process based on the information from Psychoanalysis or other information concerning the person's mental organisation.

Rhetoric Loud and confused and empty talk; "mere rhetoric". In this context the abuse of language for effect.

Schema A plan, diagram or outline, especially a mental representation of some aspect of experience, based on prior experience and memory, structured in such a way as to facilitate (and sometimes to distort) perception, recognition, the drawing of inferences or the interpretation of new information in terms of existing knowledge. (Oxford Dictionary of Psychology 2003.)

Signal Anxiety A sensation experienced when the person becomes aware that they are feeling anxious during a conversation or event even though the conversation hasn't directly addressed anything fearful or the event is not yet dangerous: they have associated something fearful with another event that may, in fact, be unrelated or distantly related.

Spreading Activation The process by which parts of the brain are stimulated by virtue of their relationship to other areas being stimulated. The effect is that excitation spreads through the brain using the relationships between neurons; these relationships may be of any form eg, proximal, learned, conceptual.

If you would like me to define my use of any other words or ideas, send me an email and when I get to the web site I will add it to the list of definitions.

Thanks for reading my book,
Cliff.

admin@realise.org or admin@acceleratedcoach.com

References

Adams, D., (1992 orig-1978) "The Hitchhiker's Guide To The Galaxy", BBCV 4751 090692 DJH LDSN
    75485 08020215 MCMXCII dir Bell, A. (orig. Radio 4)

Adams, J., (2007) "Herbartian Psychology Applied To Education", pub Kessinger

Ainsworth, M.D.S., Wittig, B. A, (1969) "Attachment And Exploratory Behaviour Of One-Year-Olds In A
    Strange Situation" in Foss, B.M. (ed) Determinants of Infant Behaviour, Vol. 4, London

Ainsworth, M. D. S., Blehar, M. C., Waters, E., & Wall, S. (1978). Patterns Of Attachment: A Psychological
    Study Of The Strange Situation. Hillsdale, N.J. Erlbaum.

Berne, E. (1964), "Games People Play", Penguin

Birdwhistell, R. L., (1970), "Kinesics And Context", U. Pennsylvania Press

Bowlby, J. (1997), "Attachment And Loss", Vol 1, Random House

Clayton, P. (2003), "Body Language At Work", Hamlyn

Collins, A.M. and Loftus, E.F. (1975), 'A Spreading Activation Theory Of Semantic Processing', Psychological
    Review, 82, pp. 407-28

Farralley, F. & Brandsma, J., (1989), 'Provocative Therapy", Meta Publications

Gick, M.l. and Holyoak, K.J. (1983) 'Schema Induction And Analogical Transfer', Cognitive Psychology, 15,
    pp.1-38.

Eagle, N., and Pentland, A., "Eigenbehaviors: Identifying Structure In Routine", Submitted to: Ubicomp '06.
    September 17-21, 2006.

Fromm, E. (1988) "The Art Of Being", Constable

Goleman, D., (1996), "Emotional Intelligence", Bloomsbury

Grinder, J. and Bandler, R. (1981) Trance Formations", Real People Press

Gross, D. M., (2006), "The Secret History Of Emotion", The University Of Chicago Press

Herbart, J. F. in Compayre, G., (2003) "Education by Instruction", University Press Pacific

Jaskolka, A., (2004), "How To Read And Use Body Language", Foulsham

Knight, S. (2002), "NLP At Work", Nicholas Brealey

Laing, R.D. (1972) "Knots", Penguin

Levine, J., Pavlidis, I., (2001), "The Lancet"

Levine, J., Pavlidis, I., Ryan, A., (2002), "Engineering In Medicine And Biology", (vol 415, p35), IEEE

Main, M. and Solomon, J. (1986) "Discovery Of Insecure/Disorganised Attachment Pattern" in Brazelton, T.
    B. and Yogman M. W. (eds) Affective Development In Infancy, Norwood, N. J., Ablex.

Marslen-Wilson, W.D. (1987) "Functional Parallelism In Spoken Word Recognition", Cognition, vol.25, no.
    1, pp.71-102

Maslow, A.H., (1957,1998), "Toward A Psychology Of Being", New York, Wiley

McClelland, J. L. and Rumelhart, D. E. (1981), 'Distributed Memory And The Representation Of General
    And Specific Information', Journal of Experimental Psychology: General, 114, pp. 159-88.

Mehrabian, A., (1968), "An Analysis Of Personality Theories", Prentice-Hall

Mehrabian, A., (1972), "Nonverbal Communication", Walter De Gruyter

Mehrabian, A., (1972), "Silent Messages: Implicit Communication of Emotions and Attitudes", Wadsworth

Mogil, M., (2003), "I Know What You're Really Thinking", Mogil, 1-4107-0261-8

Nebylitsyn, V.D., & Gray, J.A., (1972) "Biological Basis Of Individual Behaviour", Academic Press Inc

Pease, A., Pease, B., (2004), "The Definitive Book Of Body Language", Orion Books Ltd

Quick, L., (1985), "PowerPlays", Cedar

Rogers, C.R (2003, f.p 1951) "Client Centred Therapy", Constable

Rosen, S. (1991), "My Voice Will Go With You, The Teaching Tales Of Milton H. Erickson", Norton

Roth, I., Bruce, B. (1995), "Perception And Representation", Open University Press

Rumelhart, D., McClelland, J., and the PDP Research Group. (1986). Parallel Distributed Processing, Vol. I.
    Cambridge: MIT Press.

Sachs, J., Goldman, J. and Chaille, C. (1985), cited in Faulkner, (1997), "Personal, Social And Emotional Development Of Children" Ch 6 p.259, The Open University and Blackwell Press

Sacks, O., (1985), "The Man Who Mistook His Wife For A Hat", Duckworth

Schoonmaker, A. N., (1978), "Selling: The Psychological Approach", Control Data Education Company

Selman, R.I., Watts, C.I., Hickey Schultz, L, (1997), "Fostering Friendship: Pair Therapy For Treatment And Prevention (Modern Applications of Social Work)", Aldine De Gruyter New York.

Skinner, B.F. (1976), "About Behaviouism" Penguin

Stewart, I., & Joines, V., (1987), "TA Today", Lifespace

Storr, A., (1983), "The Essential Jung (Jung, K. G)", Fontana

Sun Tzu, (1995), "The Art Of War", Forward James Clavell, Hodder & Strughton

Tsien, Z., (2000), "Building a Brainer Mouse", Scientific American (April 2000)

Walther, G. R., (1992), "Power Talking (50 Ways To Say What You Mean And Get What You Want)", Berkley

Watzlawick, P. (1993 [original 1978]) "The Language Of Change", New York: W W Norton

About The Author

When Cliff started out in the 1960s he found an aptitude for computer programming that gave him access to all levels of business and business life. Later in life, he says, he 'fought' his way through a degree in psychology and worked as a teacher in business for twenty years. He is a consultant tutor on Masters' programmes, owner of a business and a father to six 'fabulous' children.

Cliff Edwards, Rift Valley, Africa 2005

Cliff has written two papers presented in: Vienna - 'Community Learning' and in Africa - 'Globalisation for the Common Good (Reconciliation)' which he co-presented with Paul McCarthy. Cliff teaches all over the world and to many of the top UK companies.

Greatest Desires: To be as good a Dad, Friend, Son and Partner I can be, to be allowed to love, to be loved and get into space at least once.

About Scanner: I thought long and hard about the structures of social interaction and their sources. After 50 years it 'came together' and I believe it can be understood; at least I want to make it easier to translate what we are saying to each other.

Interpersonal translation is a building block for interpersonal co-operation. If we add a little peace of mind, mountains of patience, a fair amount of grace and a warm heart, that might support world peace eventually and at least an increase in ambient care for each other.

"May your head protect you where your heart takes you."

(May your Cerebral cortex protect you where your Limbic system takes you?)

Notes

Notes

Notes